WORKS OF BERTOLT BRECHT

The Grove Press Edition

General Editor: Eric Bentley

Translators

Lee Baxandall

Eric Bentley

Martin Esslin

N. Goold-Verschoyle

H. R. Hays

Anselm Hollo

Christopher Isherwood

Frank Jones

Charles Laughton

Carl R. Mueller

Desmond I. Vesey

Richard Winston

Published Books

BERTOLT BRECHT

GALILEO

English Version by
CHARLES LAUGHTON

Edited and with an Introduction by
ERIC BENTLEY

GROVE PRESS
NEW YORK

Published simultaneously in Canada
Printed in the United States of America

Library of Congress Catalog Card Number 66-27699
ISBN 0-8021-3059-3

Grove Press
841 Broadway
New York, NY 10003

03 04 05 06   45 44 43 42 41 40 39 38

Contents

INTRODUCTION

Introduction

THE SCIENCE FICTION
OF BERTOLT BRECHT

Words—on a planet that is no longer in the center!
—Im Dickicht der Städte

Brecht was all wrong about the seventeenth century in general and about Galileo Galilei in particular. His main assumption is that the new cosmology gave man only a peripheral importance, where the old cosmology had given him a central one. Actually, this argument is not found in the works or conversation of Galileo, or of his friends, or of his enemies, or of anyone in his time. Discussing the point in his *Great Chain of Being,* the historian Arthur O. Lovejoy observes that the center was not held to be the place of honor anyway: prestige was out beyond the periphery, where God lived.

So much for the universe. As for the new scientific attitude, for Brecht it apparently is summed up in the pebble which his Galileo likes to drop from one hand to the other to remind himself that pebbles do not fly but fall. In short, the scientist notices, in a down-to-earth way, what actually goes on: he accepts the evidence of his senses. In this he is contrasted with the theologian, who uses imagination and reasoning. Which is all very well except that the little parable of the pebble does not characterize the stage to which physical science was brought by Galileo. It does cover his initial use of the telescope. That was a matter of looking through lenses and believing your own eyes.

However, no startling conclusions could be reached, and above all nothing could be proved, without doing a great deal more. What actually happened to physics in the seventeenth century is that it became mathematical. This meant that it became, not more concrete, but just the opposite. After all, the evidence of one's senses is that the sun goes round the earth. That the earth should go round the sun is directly counter to that evidence. The average man today accepts the latter idea on pure faith. So far as he knows, it could be wholly untrue. For the demonstration lies in the realm of the abstract and the abstruse.

Brecht is no nearer to the kind of truth that interests a biographer than he is to the kind that interests a historian of science. A good deal is known about the historical Galileo Galilei. For example, he had a mistress who bore him three children. The most human document of his biography is his correspondence with one of the daughters. The love between these two may well have been the greatest love of his life, as it certainly was of hers. But Brecht is interested in none of this, nor can it be retorted that the details of Galileo's professional life preoccupied him. Much is known of the trial of Galileo, and the material has the highest human and dramatic quality, on which various biographers have capitalized. But Brecht passes by the trial "scenes" too. Even the character of his Galileo seems only in part to have been suggested by the personality of the great scientist. The historical Galileo was a proud, possibly a vain, man. This makes him the villain of Arthur Koestler's book *The Sleepwalkers,* and, to be sure, it contributes to the villainous element in Brecht's Galileo, though Brecht is less concerned than Koestler to nag him, and more concerned to show that there are social reasons why excessive self-reliance fails to get results. Yet Galileo's self-reliance *would* have got results—as Brecht tells the story—but for a quality which Brecht has to invent* for him: cowardice. The axis of Brecht's story is passivity-activity, cowardice-courage, slyness-boldness. To make his story into a play, Brecht exploited whatever ready-made material came to hand, but must himself take full responsibility for the final product.

Would Brecht himself have admitted this, or would he have claimed that he was writing history? If I may be permitted to draw on my memory of Brecht's conversation on the point, I'd say he had a variable attitude. Sometimes he talked as if he had indeed taken everything from the historical record; other times (and this is true in the printed notes too) he would admit to changes but maintain that they didn't distort history; at other times still, he would talk as if he had an entirely free hand (as when, in 1945-46, he changed Galileo's big speech in his last scene).

Whatever Brecht thought he was doing, what good playwrights always do was perceived by Aristotle and confirmed by Lessing. When Aristotle observed that tragedy was more philosophical than history, he was noting that drama has a different logic from that of fact. History can be (or appear to be) chaotic and meaningless; drama cannot. Truth may be stranger than fiction; but it is not as orderly. Or as Pirandello stated the matter: the truth doesn't have to be plausible but fiction does. The facts of Jeanne d'Arc's life, as the historical record supplies them, did not seem to Bernard Shaw to have either plausibility or interest, for the historical Jeanne was the victim of the machinations of a vulgar politician (the historical Cauchon). The story becomes plausible and interesting by the replacement of this Cauchon with an invented one who can oppose Jeanne on principle. Now the antagonists of

---

* Or re-invent, since, certainly, Brecht is not the first writer to impute cowardice to Galileo.

Brecht's Galileo would be inconceivable had Shaw not created Warwick, Cauchon, and the Inquisitor, and, equally, Brecht's Barberini and Inquisitor could not get into his play except by replacing the Barberini and the Inquisitor of history. The historical Barberini seems to have made himself a personal enemy of Galileo, and the Inquisitor (Firenzuola) seems to have intrigued most mercilessly against him. But Brecht follows Shaw in having his protagonist's foes proceed solely from the logic of their situation. In this way the central situations of both *Saint Joan* and *Galileo* take on form and meaning. It is a paradox. The historical truth, rejected for its implausibility, has the air of an artifact, whereas the actual artifact, the play, has an air of truth. The villains of history seemed too melodramatic to both authors. The truth offended their sense of truth, and out of the less dramatic they made the more dramatic.

If what playwrights are after is fiction, why do they purport to offer us history plays at all? A teasing question, not, perhaps, to be answered without a little beating around the bush. People who ask this question generally have in mind the whole expanse of human history and envisage it all as available to the playwright. Yet a glance at history plays that have had success of any sort will reveal that they are not about the great figures of history taken indiscriminately but only about those few, like Julius Caesar, Joan of Arc, and Napoleon, whose names have become bywords. Another paradox: only when a figure has become *legendary* is he or she a good subject for a *history* play.

Are such figures as Shakespeare's Henry IV or Strindberg's Eric XIV exceptions? Not really. Within Britain, at least, the kings were legends: certainly Henry V was, as a great deal of ballad lore attests, and Henry IV is a preparation for Henry V. Something similar is true of Strindberg's histories: Swedish history was suitable for plays insofar as it was the folklore of nationalism. Because the historical dramatist is concerned with the bits of history that have stuck in people's imagination, he may well find himself handling bits of pseudo-history that are the very *product* of people's imagination. Is it likely that William Tell actually shot an apple off his son's head? What is certain is that Schiller would never have written a play about him had that story not existed.

Again, why do playwrights purport to put history on stage? Is it because the events of a history at least *seem* more real, since many spectators will assume that such a play *is* all true? After all, very much of our "knowledge" of the past is based on fiction. Did not Churchill himself claim to have learned English history from Shakespeare? Was Shakespeare's distortion of the Anglo-French quarrel just Providence's way of preparing Churchill for the Battle of Britain? So should we be prepared to see a modern, Marxist playwright distorting history in order to prepare young Communists for some future Battle of Russia? The proposition is not as remote from Bertolt Brecht's *Galileo* as it may sound. The question is whether the factual distortions have to be accepted at face value. It seems to me that even for spectators who know that a history play is bad history, such a play might still seem to have some sort of special relevancy, a more urgent truth.

Writing on Schiller's *Don Carlos,* Georg Lukács has suggested that while playwrights and novelists depart from the *facts* of history, they still present the larger *forces* of history. But the forces of what period in history, that of the ostensible action, or that of the playwright? To me it seems that the claim of the chronicle play to be close to history is valid only if it is contemporary history that is in question. *Don Carlos* belongs to the eighteenth century, not the sixteenth; Shakespeare's histories belong to the sixteenth century, not the fifteenth. Now obviously there is also an inevitable departure from the facts of the dramatist's own time. It is not even *possible* to stay close to these facts, since nothing overtly contemporary is there at all. What is it that the historical dramatist finds in the earlier period? In Brecht's terminology, it is an alienation of the subject. The familiar subject is placed in a strange setting, so that one can sit back and look and be amazed. What kind of strangeness? It is a matter of what strangeness will throw the subject into highest relief, and of what strangeness a particular writer's gift can re-create. But the strangeness is, anyhow, *only* a setting, and within the setting there must be a situation, a grouping of events, an Action, which provide a little model of what the playwright believes is going on in the present. Dramatists may spend decades looking for such settings and such Actions, or hoping to stumble on them.

Sometimes a sudden irruption of the past into the present will call the dramatist's attention to the new relevance of some old event. The canonization of Jeanne d'Arc in 1920 was such an irruption. It prompted the writing of a play which seemed to be about the age that burned Joan yet which was actually about the age that canonized her —though it would burn her if she returned. Like *Saint Joan* and all other good history plays, *Galileo* is about the playwright's own time.

Like many of Brecht's works, it exists in a number of different drafts, but it is unusual among them in taking two broadly different forms. There are two *Galileo* plays here, both of which exist in their entirety, the version of 1938, and the version of 1947. Partial analogies to the changes exist in other Brecht plays. For Brecht, it was no unique thing to create a winning rogue and then later decide to make the audience dislike him. The revisions of both *Mother Courage* and *Puntila* show this. But in *Galileo* the change was more radical.

Brecht became interested in the historical Galileo at a time when he was preoccupied with friends and comrades who remained in Germany and somehow managed to continue to work. Prominent in his thoughts was the underground political worker plotting to subvert the Hitler regime. He himself was not a "worker," he was a poet, but a poet in love with the idea of science, a poet who believed that his own philosophy was scientific: what then brings Galileo to mind?

What the mention of Galileo brings to mind is a single anecdote (incidentally, not found before 1757):

> The moment he [Galileo] was set at liberty, he looked up to the sky and down to the ground, and, stamping with his foot, in a contemplative mood, said, *Eppur si move* [sic]; that is, still it moves, meaning the earth.*

His study was the universe, and its laws are what they are, irrespective of ecclesiastical pronouncement. "Still it moves!" And Galileo can now write a new, epoch-making work, and smuggle it out of the country with these words:

> Take care when you travel through Germany with the truth under your coat!

This sentence from the first version of Brecht's *Galileo* puts in a nutshell the most striking analogy between that version of the play and the time when it was written, the 1930's, in which, indeed, truth in Germany had to be hidden under coats. It was the time when Wilhelm Reich had copies of his writings on the orgasm bound and inscribed to look like prayer books and in that form mailed from abroad to Germany. It was the time when Brecht himself wrote the essay "Writing the Truth: Five Difficulties." The fifth of these difficulties, and the one to which Brecht gave most attention, was the need of "cunning" in

---

* For further details, see *Discoveries and Opinions of Galileo*, trans. Stillman Drake (Garden City, N.Y.: Doubleday Anchor Books, 1957), p. 292.

disseminating the truth. Although Galileo is not included in the essay's list of heroes who showed such cunning, the whole passage is quite close to the thought and frame of mind reflected in the first version of the Galileo play. Even the special perspective which caused Brecht's friend Walter Benjamin to say its hero was not Galileo but the people is found in such sentences as: "Propaganda that stimulates thinking, in no matter what field, is useful to the cause of the oppressed." The early version of *Galileo* is nothing if not propaganda for thinking.

The later version of *Galileo* is also about the playwright's own time, but this was now, not the 1930's, but the mid-1940's. Brecht has himself recorded what the motive force of the new *Galileo* was:

> The atomic age made its debut at Hiroshima in the middle of our work. Overnight the biography of the founder of the new system of physics read differently.

To a historian it would seem bizarre to suggest that he should reverse a judgment he had made on something in the seventeenth century on account of something which had just happened in the twentieth. To a dramatist, however, the question would mainly be whether a subject which had suggested itself because it resembled something in the twentieth century would still be usable when asked to resemble something quite different in the twentieth century.

In the 1930's, as I have been saying, what presumably commended the subject of Galileo to Brecht was the analogy between the seventeenth-century scientist's underground activities and those of twentieth-century leftwingers in Hitler Germany. But that is not all that Brecht, even in the early version, made of the *exemplum*. The abjuration was defined as an act of cowardice, and the act of cowardice was then deplored for a precise reason, namely, that more than certain notions about astronomy were at stake—at stake was the liberty to advance these and any other notions:

> ANDREA: . . . many on all sides followed you with their eyes and ears, believing that you stood, not only for a particular view of the movement of the stars, but even more for the liberty of teaching—in all fields. Not then for any particular thoughts, but for the right to think at all. Which is in dispute. When these people heard what you had said *abjured,* it seemed to them not only that certain thoughts about the movements of the stars had been discredited, but that thinking itself, which is regarded as unholy when it operates with reasons and proofs, had been discredited.

> VIRGINIA: But it is not true that the authorities have forbidden the sciences, as just stated. Father Philip says the Church will include my father's great inventions and discoveries in the textbooks. Only theology, which is quite a different science—there he should not take issue with their views.

> GALILEO: In free hours, of which I have many, I have wondered how my conduct must look to that scientific community to which I of course no longer belong, even though I am still acquainted with some of its modes of thought. (*Speaking as on an academic occasion, his hands folded over his belly*:) It will have to ponder whether it can be satisfied that its members deliver to it a certain number of propositions, let us say about the tendencies of falling bodies or the movements of certain stars. I have shut myself off, as was said, from the scientific way of thought, but I assume that, faced with the danger of annihilation, science will hardly be in a position to release its members from all further obligations. For example, the obligation to contribute to its own continuance as science. Even a wool merchant, aside from buying cheap and delivering decent wool, can also be concerned that trading in wool is permitted at all and is able to proceed. Accordingly, then, a member of the scientific

community cannot logically just point to his possible merits as a researcher if he has neglected to honor his profession as such and to defend it against coercion of every kind. But this is a business of some scope. For science demands that facts not be subordinated to opinions but that opinions be subordinated to facts. It is not in a position to limit these propositions and apply them to "some" opinions and "such and such" facts. To be certain that these propositions can always and without limitation be acted on, science must do battle to ensure that they are respected in all fields.

After Hiroshima, Brecht deleted these speeches, in order to substitute another idea. The point was no longer to demand from the authorities liberty to teach all things but to demand from the scientists themselves a sense of social responsibility, a sense of identification with the destiny, not of other scientists only, but of people at large. The point was now to dissent from those who see scientific advance as "an end in itself," thus playing into the hands of those who happen to be in power, and to advance the alternate, utilitarian conception of science:

> GALILEO: . . . I take it that the intent of science is to ease human existence. If you give way to coercion, science can be crippled, and your new machines may simply suggest new drudgeries. Should you, then, in time, discover all there is to be discovered, your progress must become a progress away from the bulk of humanity. The gulf might even grow so wide that the sound of your cheering at some new achievement would be echoed by a universal howl of horror.

In this respect, *Galileo I* is a "liberal" defense of freedom against tyranny, while *Galileo II** is a Marxist defense of

---

* These are perhaps the handiest terms to describe the two broadly different texts of the play. It is *Galileo II* that is found in the collected plays as published by Suhrkamp Verlag

a social conception of science against the "liberal" view that truth is an end in itself.

If this philosophic change is large enough, it is accompanied by an even larger change in the dramatic action. In *Galileo I,* a balance is struck between two opposing motifs. On the one hand, Galileo is admired for his slyness and cunning, while on the other being condemned for his cowardice. The admiration is never entirely swallowed up in the disapproval. On the contrary, we give Galileo a good mark for conceding his own weakness. Then, too, Brecht brings about a partial rehabilitation of his hero in two distinct ways: first, by stressing the admirable cunning of the underground worker who can write a new masterpiece under these conditions and arrange to smuggle it out to freer lands; second, by defining his hero's lapse as a limited one, thus:

> ANDREA: . . . it is as if a very high tower which had been thought indestructible should fall to the ground. The noise of its collapse was far louder than the din of the builders and the machines had been during the whole period of its construction. And the pillar of dust which the collapse occasioned rose higher than the tower had ever done. But possibly it turns out, when the dust clears, that, while twelve top floors have fallen, thirty floors below are still standing. Is that what you mean? There is this to be said for it: the things that are wrong in this

---

(Frankfurt, 1957). The Methuen edition of Brecht's plays contains a translation of *Galileo II* by Desmond I. Vesey. The Laughton text is also a translation of *Galileo II,* but with omissions and some differences in detail. *Galileo I* has not been published in any language. There is an unpublished translation by Desmond I. Vesey. The German original of *Galileo I* was made available to me by Mr. Arvid Englind, in whose name it was copyrighted in 1940. Quotations from *Galileo II* will be in the Laughton version, except when the passage quoted has been omitted from it. In that case, I have translated from the German.

science of ours are out in the open. . . . The difficulty
may be the greater; but the necessity has also become
greater.

And indeed there is something good about the new book's
having a disgraced author, namely, that it must now
make its way on its own, and not by authority; which
will be a gain for science and the scientific community.
And dramatically it means a lot that *Galileo I* ends with
the emphasis on the renewal of friendship between
Galileo and Andrea. The old scientist is after all able
to hand his work on, as to a son.

Revising the play after Hiroshima, Brecht decided to
condemn Galileo far more strongly, and in fact not only
to render an unqualified verdict of guilty, but also to picture a shipwrecked, a totally corrupted human being. The
sense of the earlier text is: I should not have let my fear
of death make me overlook the fact that I had something
more to defend than a theory in pure astronomy. The
sense of the later text is: To be a coward in those circumstances entailed something worse than cowardice itself,
namely, treachery. In the early text, Brecht alludes to the
Church's belief that Galileo risked damnation for squan-
dering the gift of intellect. In the later text, it is clear that
Galileo sees himself as already in Hell for having actually
squandered (i.e., betrayed) the gift of intellect. And so
what we see in the penultimate scene of the later text is a
portrait of a "collaborator," a renegade. And Brecht's
notes* stress that Galileo should register a malign, mis-

---

* Some of Brecht's notes on *Galileo* are provided in the
Suhrkamp and Methuen editions of the play. Others are given
in *Aufbau einer Rolle: Galilei,* the three-volume presentation
of the play published by Henschelverlag in East Berlin (1958).
Suhrkamp has also published a separate volume of notes on
Galileo which are not limited to either of these two previous
sources (*Materialien zu Brechts "Leben des Galilei,"* 1963).

anthropic contempt for Federzoni, as well as shouting in sheer self-hatred to Andrea:

> Welcome to my gutter, dear colleague in science and brother in treason: I sold out, you are a buyer. . . . Blessed be our bargaining, whitewashing, death-fearing community!

Which version is better? There can be no doubt that many small improvements were made throughout the play by which the later version benefited. But as far as this penultimate scene is concerned, it is not clear that, in making it more ambitious, Brecht also improved it. To show the foulness of Galileo's crime, he has to try to plumb deeper depths. The question is whether this befouled, denatured Galileo can be believed to be the same man we have seen up to then. The impression is, rather, of someone Brecht arbitrarily declares bad at this stage in order to make a point. Which would be of a piece with Communist treatment of the Betrayal theme generally. One moment, a Tito is a Jesus, and the next, a Judas. There is, perhaps, an intrusion of unfelt Communist clichés about traitors and renegades in the later *Galileo*. One cannot find, within the boundaries of the play itself, a full justification for the virulence of the final condemnation.

If the crime of Galileo, in the earlier text, being less cataclysmic in its results and less anguished in its style, at first seems less dramatic, it is actually rendered *more* dramatic by the tragicomic relationship in which it stands to Galileo's Schweykian cunning. Personally I find the ambiguity of the earlier ending more human and more richly dramatic, as well as more Brechtian and more consistent with the rest of the play.

Sidelights are provided by performances of the play, and their background. It seems to me that even Ernst Busch, the Galileo of the Berlin Ensemble production, could not make real the image of a corrupted Galileo.

Busch was very much the Old Communist. The danger was that he might have been just that and never Galileo Galilei. He never seemed the sinner in Hell, but, rather, the Party Member who had strayed and was now practicing Self-Criticism. Charles Laughton would seem a likelier casting. Brecht said Laughton felt guilty for having stayed in Hollywood during World War II instead of returning to fight for Britain, and this sense of guilt, he said, was what would come in useful in Galileo. Laughton did indeed have subtly personal ways of making guilt seem real that would have delighted Stanislavsky himself. When he made his entrance after the abjuration, he seemed, as Brecht said, a little boy who had wet his pants, but, in his last scene, when Brecht wanted the audience to reject Galileo in horror, Laughton made sure they accepted him in pity —while loving him at the same time for the way he out-witted the Inquisition. In other words, the actor put some-thing of Galileo I back into Galileo II. Perhaps it is hard not to. The action (Galileo smuggling his new book out) is apt, in a theatre, to speak louder than mere words of denunciation. But then again, the way in which Laughton "stood out" from his part was not exactly what the Brech-tian theory bargains for. For it was through an actorish narcissism that he kept aloof; and this limited his power to communicate the content of the play. It also made the sinister and self-defeating pride of the scientist dwindle into a movie star's showy and nervous vanity. Laughton had a unique equipment for this role. It is unlikely that anyone again will combine as he did every appearance of intellectual brilliance with every appearance of physical self-indulgence. But actorish vanity allowed him to let the brilliance slide over into drawing-room-comedy smart-ness. Narcissism prevented him from even trying to enter those somewhat Dostoevskian depths into which Brecht invites the actor of the penultimate scene, version two.

Brecht added a detail in the later text which might

help a great deal to define that "tragedy of pride" which is certainly a part of this drama. Galileo is offered a conceivable way of escape—the patronage of the iron founder Matti. But he is not an astute enough politician to get the point, and prefers to believe not only in the authorities themselves but in his own ability to go it alone. Laughton, by not seeming to take in what Matti was saying, threw this little scene away. The effect was not of arrogant overconfidence but merely of lack of rapport or maybe—again —trivial vanity. (Perhaps Brecht learned from this. The Suhrkamp-Methuen text gives a yet later version of the scene, in which the iron founder, now an industrialist called Vanni, explicitly offers himself as an alternative to the Inquisition and is explicitly turned down.)

It was also through Charles Laughton that the notion was first spread around that *Galileo* not only touches on the atom bomb but is essentially concerned with it. Here is Brecht himself in this vein:

> Galileo's crime can be regarded as the original sin of modern physical science. . . . The atom bomb, both as a technical and as a social phenomenon, is the classical end product of his contribution to science and his failure to society.

But such a meaning does not emerge from the story as told either by historians or by Brecht. Had those who wished to stop Galileo and scientific advance had their way, there would be no atom bomb. Conversely, if we accept the Brechtian premise that Galileo could have changed history by making an opposite decision, then he would have changed history by joining hands with Matti-Vanni the industrialist, and the atom bomb might have been invented a little earlier—say, by Wernher von Braun.

In East Berlin, 1965, Heinar Kipphardt's play about J. Robert Oppenheimer began in the setting left on stage from Brecht's *Galileo,* and the newer play "shows what society exacts from its individuals, what it needs from them," as Brecht said his *Galileo* did. However, one is struck by the extreme difference between the two main dramatic situations—that in which it is Reaction that suppresses discovery, and that in which it was inhumane to push *for* science and the *making* of a discovery.

One American production of Brecht's *Galileo*, at my suggestion, posted up the following words for the audience to read after the abjuration scene:

> I was not in a policy-making position at Los Alamos.
> I would have done anything that I was asked to do.
> —J. ROBERT OPPENHEIMER

But I now think there is sensationalism in this idea, for Galileo has not offered to do "anything" he might be "asked to do" at all. And dramatically it makes a big difference that he is not being asked to do something but being asked not to do something. He is being asked not to pursue his researches. Then he goes and pursues them anyway, muttering, "Eppur si muove."

The story to which the Oppenheimer dossier leads, when interpreted by a Marxist, is told, not in Brecht's *Galileo*, but in Haakon Chevalier's novel, *The Man Who Would Be God*. Here the faith the protagonist stands for is obviously Marxism. He betrays it and his best friend (who is also his best Comrade) in order to become the man who can make Reaction a gift of the atom bomb. The ending resembles *Galileo II* to the extent that both protagonists are shown as burnt-out ruins of their former selves; but Chevalier's man does not practice Self-Criticism.

Chevalier makes it clear he thinks the Action of his story describes a curve like that of Greek tragedy; and this curve may suggest, too, the Action of Brecht's play. The rhythm of both, we might at first think, is: from battle to defeat, loyalty to betrayal, commitment to alienation. But to write religious tracts for a cardinal, as Galileo did, is not to devise a monstrous weapon, as Oppenheimer did. For one thing, while it is quite credible that devising a monstrous weapon would give a man delusions of satanic grandeur, thus corrupting him, Galileo's obligation to turn out a little conformist journalism is merely a boring chore.

It is true that *Galileo II* touches, or almost touches, on many of the problems which were created or augmented by the atomic bomb—and this has legitimately been stressed by the judicious H. E. Rank in defending Brecht against a charge of unseriousness made by Nigel Dennis.* Still, even *Galileo II* is based, not on Oppenheimer folklore, but on Galileo folklore, and a preoccupation with the similarities, by blinding critics to the enormous differences, is, in my view, a disservice to Brecht the dramatist. It prevents the Action as a whole from being perceived. If we begin by assuming that the play is about the atomic scientists, we shall end by complaining that Brecht doesn't get to the point till very near the end.

If *Galileo* is not "all about the atom bomb," is it a tragedy of pride? One might begin to answer this question with the observation that no tragedy of pride would end in its hero's lacking, not only pride, but even self-respect. At the end, supremely, the true hero reveals his true heroism, and if lack of self-respect has been in question, as in Conrad's *Lord Jim,* then what he will do with his self-respect at the end is precisely to regain it. *Galileo* (*I* or *II*) is more of a tragedy of *lack* of pride; but that, to be sure, is no tragedy at all. Brecht himself, speaking of his play in terms of a commitment abandoned and betrayed, indicates that he has nothing against writers like Copernicus, who never made a commitment. Copernicus simply left his book for men to make of it what they would after his death. Galileo embarked on a campaign to change the world, then quit.

---

* Dennis's piece is in *Encounter,* October, 1960, Rank's in *Stand,* Vol. V, No. 1 (n.d.).

Brecht shows the trend of his own thinking about the play
by the use of words like "opportunism," "collaboration,"
"betrayal." To these one must add the equally Brechtian
term "capitulation." To begin full of fighting spirit, to end
capitulating ignominiously: this is the rhythm of life as
Brecht so often depicted it, and so deeply felt it. In *Mother
Courage,* the "great" capitulation—Courage's own—is over
before the first curtain rises. We find it only in certain
speeches and a retrospective song. In *Galileo,* on the other
hand, it is the hinge of the whole Action. The play is
a tragicomedy of heroic combat followed by unheroic
capitulation, and the ending of the later version is of the
harrowing sort common in tragicomedy when it achieves
greatness: no noble contrition, no belated rebellion even,
but savage, misanthropic self-hatred. This Galileo is the
victim of his own curse upon Mucius:*

> A man who doesn't know the truth is just an idiot, but a
> man who knows the truth and calls it a lie is a crook.

Received "into the ranks of the faithful," he is exiled from
the ranks of mankind, *and that by his own decree.*

That the horror of the self-denunciation scene did not

---

* Reference is to a page or so of Scene 9 in the published
German text which is not in the Laughton version (Scene 8).
Mucius is a scientist who, after studying mathematics with
Galileo, sides with the Church against him. The brief con-
frontation ends thus:

GALILEO: And don't talk about problems! I didn't permit the
plague to stop me continuing my research.

MUCIUS: Mr. Galilei, the plague is not the worst.

GALILEO: Let me tell you this. A man who doesn't know
the truth is just an idiot, but a man who knows the truth
and calls it a lie is a crook. Get out of here!

MUCIUS (*in a toneless voice*): You are right. (*Exit.*)

fully emerge in the 1947 production Brecht was inclined to blame on Laughton. It was one of the few passages, he says in his notes, which the actor had difficulties with. He did not seem, Brecht continues, to grasp the playwright's plea that a condemnation of the opportunist must be inherent in the condemnation of those who accept the fruits of the opportunism. Not using the squint-eyed, worried grin he had worn in the abjuration scene, Laughton here robbed the opening of the big speech on science of its superciliousness:

> It·did not entirely emerge that you are on the lowest rung of the ladder of teaching when you deride the ignorant and that it is a hateful light which a man emits just to have his own light shine . . .

Laughton failed to make his audiences feel that "that man sits in a Hell worse than Dante's where the gift of intellect has been gambled away."

But could not Laughton be partly excused for not playing what Brecht calls the low point of the Action on the grounds that this low point is hardly reached in the writing? When we ask this we are asking a question not only about the dialogue of the penultimate scene but also about the scene that sets it up: the abjuration scene. This scene represents an extreme instance of Brechtian method. Brecht well knew that the obvious way to write this scene was to confront Galileo with his enemies. Some playwrights would make you sit there three hours for the sole pleasure of seeing this happen at the end.* Brecht's reason for doing

---

* Not a mere speculation. The only Galileo play I have read that precedes Brecht's is by the nineteenth-century French dramatist François Ponsard. Ponsard's final curtain line is: "Et pourtant elle tourne!" I doubt very much that Brecht had read Ponsard, but, if he had, one would be able to say he took the older work and stood it on its head (or feet) in his usual fashion. Ponsard gives us a wholly noble Galileo and

otherwise is clear: the people he wishes to confront Galileo with are—his friends. In the theatre, it is a truly marvelous scene, with its off-stage action, its two groups waiting on stage (the friends and the daughter), its climactic, anticlimactic entrance of Galileo Galilei, the collapse of Andrea, and the laconic, meaning-packed summing up of Galileo's retort to him: "Unhappy is the land that *needs* a hero!" This line has a partly new meaning in *Galileo II*, being now far more ironical, yet it contains a direct, unironic truth still, expressing, as Brecht says, the scientist's wish to deprive Nature of her privilege of making life tragic and heroism necessary. Yet the scene is perhaps a shade *too* oblique. One senses the presence of an intention which is not entirely achieved: to avoid the hackneyed, overprepared climax of conventional drama in the big, long trial scene by bringing down the hero with a flick of the wrist. The abjuration is there before one is ready for it. Our man collapses without a fight. Something is gained. There is a special interest in collapse being so prompt, so sudden, so actionless, after all the overconfidence that had gone before. The Brechtian avoidance of psychology does pay off here in shock. But I wonder if it doesn't force the playwright to omit something we need at once for continuity of narrative and later for our understanding of Galileo's descent into hatred of himself and contempt for others?

To condemn Galileo for his abjuration, one must be-

---

is at pains to free the scientist from the *possible* charge of cowardice. He confronts Galileo with a tragic choice between Science and Family: as a noble hero, he must of course choose the latter. The Family is represented by his daughter; and so concern for his daughter's welfare becomes the high cause for which he suffers. How tempting to conclude that Brecht did read Ponsard and decided on the spot to have his Galileo ride roughshod over his daughter's happiness! And so on.

lieve, first, that he had a real alternative and, second, that this alternative was worth all the trouble. Thirdly, his enemies must be as convincing in their way as he is in his, or the whole conflict lacks the magnitude it could have. Now, to take the last point first, the enemy figures in *Galileo*, though done with adroitness, are markedly less impressive than those they are roughly modeled on—the enemies in *Saint Joan*. As to Galileo's alternative, the trouble is not that we may feel asked to believe that the *historical* Galileo had such an alternative, the trouble is that, unless we can see all history and society in these terms of progressives and reactionaries, we shall not respond as Brecht would like us to. Faced with this kind of objection, Brecht used to say that *all* plays require agreement with the author's philosophy. But do they? Don't they require, rather, only a suspension of disbelief, a temporary willingness to see things through the playwright's spectacles? And is that the issue, here, anyway? Could not the terms of this conflict be objected to on the grounds of the very philosophy Brecht did accept, Marxism? It seems to me that a Marxist should object that the dialectic of history and society is here excessively attenuated. The result is a melodramatic simplification. And the fact that this story cannot be thought of as actually taking place in the seventeenth century does become a dramatic defect *by being called attention to*. In this it resembles the story of Mother Courage, who is condemned for what she did, though what she ought to have done instead (namely, helped to destroy the system) was not in the seventeenth-century cards. There is something absurd, then, in condemning her, and there is something absurd in asking Galileo Galilei to strike a blow for the philosophy of Bertolt Brecht. If Cardinal and Inquisitor are abstract and simplistic, so is the play's rendering of the alternative to them, as shown in the character of Federzoni, the idealized worker. *Federzoni is made of wood,* and so, even more obviously, are various smaller characters, introduced to make points, like Mucius the Renegade and Matti-Vanni the Businessman. Before Galileo is arrested, Brecht offers him through Matti-Vanni the alternative of working for the rising bourgeoisie. The point is made, but only by being mentioned, as it might be mentioned in an essay. It does not register as drama, because Matti exercises no pull on Galileo; he is a mere mouthpiece.

These weaknesses would be cruelly displayed by any director who labored under the misapprehension that this was a Shaw play. *Galileo* can suffer by being compared to *Saint Joan* in that Shaw puts much more thought into drama and finds much more drama in thought. *Saint Joan,* on the other hand, might suffer a little by comparison with *Galileo* if what one was after was not thinking but poetry —whether the poetry of the word or the poetry of stage-craft.

"The hero is the people." Walter Benjamin's hyperbole applies, not to the prosaically imposed "vulgar" Marxism of the Federzoni figure, but to the impact of Galileo's life upon the commonalty, a topic to which two whole scenes are devoted—the carnival scene and the last scene of the play, in which Andrea is seen leaving Italy. The people are the hero in that the final interest is not in Galileo himself but in what he did, and what he failed to do, *for* the people. And here objections on historical grounds—that the seventeenth-century populace did not react in this way, that Galileo wrote in Italian instead of Latin, not to reach the people, who couldn't read, but to reach the middle class —cannot be upheld, because the poet has created a vision that transcends literal reportage. The carnival scene usually goes over better with an audience than any other scene in the play. Cynics may say that is because it is a creation of the director and composer. The design remains Brecht's own. The little scene gives us an image that resembles the image of Azdak in *The Caucasian Chalk Circle*. In each case, the common folk, in their lóng night of slavery, are given a brief glimpse of a possible dawn, and Brecht is able to convey this, not discursively, but in direct, poetic-dramatic vision.

And, of course, it is a matter, not just of a scene, but of the whole play. As we work our way back from the last scene, through the scene of abjuratíon, to the long preparation for the abjuration scene, we can discern the curve of the whole Action. One might find the key to this Action in the phrase "the New Age." It is a favorite Brechtian topic, and Brecht explains in his notes to *Galileo* that the phrase "the New Age" brought to his mind the Workers' Movement as of the beginning of the twentieth century:

> . . . no other line from a song so powerfully inspired the workers as the line, "Now a new age is dawning": old and young marched to it. . . .

This is the theme that is sounded in the very first scene of *Galileo,* and again I wish to make a somewhat more than parenthetic allusion to Charles Laughton, since here Laughton the adapter conspired with Laughton the actor to evade an important issue. The actor found the speech about the New Age far too long, so the adapter cut most of it out, and had the remainder rebuked by an Andrea who says: "You're off again, Mr. Galilei." But it was Mr. Brecht who was off again, and a really long speech is needed here, a veritable paean to the idea of a New Age, or we cannot grasp the importance of the conception or the sentiment in the main design. The paean is a poem, though in prose:

> GALILEO: Walls and crystal spheres and immobility! For two thousand years mankind believed that the sun and all the stars of heaven turned around them. The Pope,

the cardinals, the princes, scholars, captains, merchants, fishwives and schoolchildren thought they were sitting, stationary, in this crystal globe. But now we're emerging from it, Andrea.

For the old age is through, and a new age is upon us. During hundreds of years it has been as if mankind awaited something.

The cities are narrow, and so are brains. Superstitions and plague. But now the word is: since it is so, it does not remain so. For everything moves, my friend.

On our old continent a rumor has arisen: there are new continents. And since our ships have sailed to them, the saying circulates on the laughing continents: the great, much-dreaded ocean is just a puddle.

And men have come to take great pleasure in searching out the causes of all things: why the stone falls when it is dropped, and how it rises when it is thrown into the air.

Every day something is found. Even the centenarians have the young shout in their ears what new thing has been discovered. Much has been found already, but more can be found in the future. And so there is still much for new generations to do. The old teachings, believed for a thousand years, are on the point of collapsing. There is less wood in the beams of these structures than in the supports which are supposed to hold them up. But the new knowledge is a new building of which only the scaffolding is there. Even the teaching of the great Copernicus is not yet proved. But mankind will soon be properly informed as to its dwelling place, the heavenly body where it has its home. What is written in the old books does not satisfy mankind any more.

For where Belief has sat for a thousand years, there today sits Doubt. All the world says: yes, that is written in the books, but now let us see for ourselves.

The most celebrated truths are tapped on the shoulder. What never was doubted is doubted now.

And thereby a wind has arisen which blows up the

gold-brocaded cloaks of princes and prelates, so that fat or skinny legs are seen beneath, legs like our legs.

The skies, it has turned out, are empty. Men laugh merrily at that.

But the water of the earth drives the new distaffs, and five hundred hands are busy in the rope and sail shops at the dockyards making a New Order.

Even the sons of fishwives go to school. In the markets, the new stars are talked about.

It was always said that the stars were fastened to a crystal vault so that they could not fall. Now we have taken heart and let them float in the air, without support, and they are embarked on a great voyage—like us, who are also without support and embarked on a great voyage.

But the universe lost its center overnight, and in the morning it had a countless number of centers. So that now each one can be regarded as a center and none can. For there is a lot of room suddenly.

Our ships sail on far seas, our stars move in far space. In chess the rooks can now be moved right across the board.

So that the poet says: "O early dawn of the beginning! O breath of the wind that comes from newfound shores!"*

This speech creates a sense of that Enchantment which will later, as the very climax of the Action, turn to Disenchantment (ambiguously in one version, unequivocally in the other). In *The Caucasian Chalk Circle,* we learn how much too early the carpet weavers tried to establish a people's regime, and for how short a time Azdak's people's regime can eke out its fluky existence. In *Galileo,* the point is that the coming of such a regime is actually postponed by the protagonist's principal act. And though we cannot take this as history (of the seventeenth century), we can

---

*From *Galileo I.* The sentence about the rooks seems to be based on the erroneous belief that in former times the rooks could move only one square at a time.

certainly make sense of it as politics (of the twentieth century).

It has become customary to cut the last scene, but this is because directors insist on believing that Galileo is the hero. If the people are the hero, the last scene is a needed conclusion and a needed correction of the carnival scene. The people will not emerge into the dawn in the sudden ecstasy of Carnival. The journey out of night is long and slow, all the slower because of Galileo's abjuration and all analogous capitulations. At the end, the play abuts upon the Marxist realization that the people must learn not to rely on the Great Men of the bourgeoisie for their salvation: they will have to save themselves. But discreetly enough, this is not spelled out. Brecht speaks here through image and action.

In *Galileo II* the smuggling out of the new book has a meaning somewhat different from what it had in *Galileo I*. It is less of a triumph for Galileo, but it does take up the theme of *eppur si muove* and partially redeem it from the cynicism which, especially in this version, it must carry. The earth continues to revolve, and even the bad man can continue to contribute good science. Or, on a more literal plane: though a social setback is recorded, science marches ahead—in which contrast, that between a rotten society and a flourishing science, we again glimpse the twentieth century.

A further comment is perhaps needed on the protagonist of Brecht's play. What does this Galileo—as against the Galileo of the historians—finally amount to? The topic can conveniently be approached through the following passage from Isaac Deutscher's life of Trotsky:

> He [Brecht] had been in some sympathy with Trotskyism and was shaken by the purges; but he could not bring himself to break with Stalinism. He surrendered to it with a load of doubt on his mind, as the capitulators in Russia had done; and he expressed artistically his and

their predicament in *Galileo Galilei*. It was through the prism of the Bolshevik experience that he saw Galileo going down on his knees before the Inquisition and doing this from an "historic necessity," because of the people's political and spiritual immaturity. The Galileo of his drama is Zinoviev or Bukharin or Rakovsky dressed up in historical costume. He is haunted by the "fruitless" martyrdom of Giordano Bruno; that terrible example causes him to surrender to the Inquisition, just as Trotsky's fate caused so many Communists to surrender to Stalin. And Brecht's famous duologue: "Happy is the country that produces such a hero" and 'Unhappy is the people that needs such a hero" epitomizes clearly enough the problem of Trotsky and Stalinist Russia rather than Galileo's quandary in Renaissance Italy. (Brecht wrote the original version of *Galileo Galilei* in 1937-38, at the height of the Great Purges.)

Unless Mr. Deutscher has his hands on some version of *Galileo* not known by the rest of us to exist he can't read straight. *Galileo II cannot* be taken the way he proposes, since the capitulation, there, is denounced as loudly as he could wish. If we assume, as perhaps we must, that it is *Galileo I* he is talking about, then how could he take the Church (Stalinism) to be something Galileo "could not bring himself to break with," in view of the fact that his Galileo cheats and outwits the Church triumphantly? Maybe Mr. Deutscher never got to the penultimate scene. Brecht's Galileo is not haunted by the martyrdom of Bruno, either, and if Bruno is Trotsky, then Trotsky hardly comes within the purview of the play at all. And does Mr. Deutscher take "Happy is the country that produces such a hero" to be about Trotsky? If so, inaccuracy has again tripped him up, as the line actually reads: "Unhappy is the land that breeds no hero!" and the reference is to Galileo's failure to be heroic.

But Mr. Deutscher's incursion into dramatic criticism raises the question whether he claims to describe Brecht' conscious thoughts or things that crept in, in the author's despite. If the former, then the Deutscher thesis is highly implausible. Brecht may have been troubled by inner doubts,* but on the whole he seems to have given his approval to the Moscow trials, much in the spirit of his close friend Feuchtwanger, whose ardently Stalinist book *Moscow, 1937* is mentioned by Mr. Deutscher. Besides, the abjuration in *Galileo I* is in part a means to an end, which is to go on writing subversive things. Though reprehensible, it is also a neat trick, and no occasion for Slavic breast-beating. That Brecht would knowingly have depicted Stalin as the enemy is, on the evidence available so far, improbable.

Yet it may well be true that not only the Nazi but the Bolshevik experience found their way into the play, especially into its later version, which Mr. Deutscher doesn't seem to have read. The Communist idea of self-criticism, going to all possible lengths of self-denunciation and a demand for punishment, undoubtedly exerted considerable sway over Brecht. In 1943-45, he is using it in *The Caucasian Chalk Circle*, in a passage so "Russian" that Western audiences have trouble following the argument. If we are now guessing at unconscious motives, instead of just noting the provable ones, we might by all means guess that the self-denunciation of the new version of *Galileo*, written in 1945 or so, was put there to correct and place in proper perspective the famous self-denunciation before the Inquisition, around which the story is built. The abjuration is a spurious piece of self-denunciation. It cries out, Brecht might well have felt, for a real one. And the real one, by all means, suggests the world of Zinoviev, Bukharin, and Rakovsky. However, if this interpretation is valid, Brecht's unconscious made, surely, the same identification as his

* A poem published in 1964 could be cited in evidence. The title is: "Are the People Infallible?" My translation appears in *Tulane Drama Review*, X, No. 4 (Summer, 1966), 64-77.

conscious mind, namely with Stalin, not with his enemies, who are felt to be guilty as charged.

But wasn't the Nazi experience far more important to the play than the Bolshevik one? The real complaint against Galileo is that he did not rise up like Georgi Dimitrov at the Reichstag trial in Leipzig and denounce his judges. The real complaint is against German physicists who announced that there was such a thing as Aryan physics as distinct from Jewish physics. The real complaint is against the conspiracy of silence in which most German scholars and writers took part in those years. Brecht's poetry of the 1930's reverts again and again to this subject.

> Aber man wird nicht sagen: Die Zeiten waren finster
> Sondern: Warum haben ihre Dichter geschwiegen?

> But men won't say: The times were dark,
> But: Why were their poets silent?

And Brecht's personal relation to this subject? He was by no means silent, but he knew how to take care of himself. He did not volunteer in Spain. He did not go to Moscow to risk his neck at the headquarters of Revolution. And undoubtedly such guilt as was felt (if any was) by Charles Laughton at not taking part in the Battle of Britain was felt by Brecht a thousand times over at not taking more than a literary part in *any* of the battles of his lifetime. This guilt, one can readily believe, is concentrated in the protagonist in whose footsteps some people think Brecht trod when before the Un-American Activities Committee he cried, "No, no, no, no, no, never," at the question: "Have you ever made application to join the Communist Party?"

"The sick inmost being of a poet," Jean Paul has it, "betrays itself nowhere more than in his hero, whom he never fails to stain with the secret weaknesses of his own nature." Brecht felt in himself a natural affinity with the shirker and the "quitter." In that respect *Galileo*, a late play, looks all the way back to the earliest plays, and especially to *Drums in the Night*. A whole row of Brecht protagonists belongs to this species in one way or another (Baal, Galy Gay, Macheath, Mother Courage, Schweyk, Azdak . . .)* and what gives these figures dramatic tension is that their natural passivity has either to be redeemed by the addition of some other quality (as with Schweyk's intuitive shrewdness and humanity) or worked up into something much worse that can be roundly denounced. This working up took Brecht a little time, as we know from the revisions of *Mother Courage* and *Puntila*. It was a

---

* To this list, except that he is not the protagonist of a play, belongs Herr Keuner. And interestingly enough, Brecht introduced into *Galileo I* a complete "Keuner story," thus: "Into the home of the Cretan philosopher Keunos, who was beloved among the Cretans for his love of liberty, came one day, during the time of tyranny, a certain agent, who presented a pass that had been issued by those who ruled the city. It said that any home he set foot in belonged to him; likewise, any food he demanded; likewise, any man should serve him that he set eyes on. The agent sat down, demanded food, washed, lay down, and asked, with his face toward the wall, before he fell asleep: 'Will you serve me?' Keunos covered him with a blanket, drove the flies away, watched over his sleep, and obeyed him for seven years just as on this day. But whatever he did for him, he certainly kept from doing one thing, and that was to utter a single word. When the seven years were up, and the agent had grown fat from much eating, sleeping, and commanding, the agent died. Keunos then wrapped him in the beat-up old blanket, dragged him out of the house, washed the bed, whitewashed the walls, took a deep breath, and answered: 'No.' " The speech is given to Galileo in Scene 8, and Brecht is able thereby to differentiate Galileo from Andrea, in preparation for later scenes: "(*The pupils laugh. Only Andrea shakes his head.*) ANDREA: I don't like the story, Mr. Galilei."

quarter of a century before Brecht made it clear that Kragler, of *Drums in the Night*, was to be utterly rejected. And, of course, the wholehearted rejection of Galileo's "crime" took Brecht some eight years to make—eight years and two atom bombs. Brecht, one might put it, was a moralist on second thought, and, however moralist-critics may judge him as a man, they can hardly deny that this "contradiction" in him was dramatically dynamic and productive.

Galileo is a self-portrait in respect of incarnating the main contradiction of Brecht's own personality. That can hardly fail to have interest for students of his work. But it can hardly be the main point of *Galileo,* if we judge *Galileo* to be a good play, since good plays are not, in the first or last instance, personal outpourings. A writer writes himself, but a playwright has written a play only when he has written more than, or other than, himself. Even should his material stem from himself, the test is whether he can get it outside himself and make it not-himself. He has to let himself be strewn about like dragon's teeth so that other men may spring up, armed. In *Galileo,* a contradiction that had once merely been Brecht's own—had been, then, merely a character trait—is translated into action, into an Action, and this action, reciprocally, attaches itself to someone who is neither Bertolt Brecht nor the Galileo Galilei of history. Though he bear the latter's name, he is a *creation* of the former, and surely a very notable one. It is not just that Brecht's Galileo is contradictory. Such a contradiction would count for comparatively little if the *man* who is contradictory were not both deeply, complexly human and —great. Nor is greatness, in plays, taken on trust or proved by citation of the evidence. Rather, it must be there as a visible halo, and felt as an actual charisma. As the man speaks, moves, or merely stands there, his greatness must, for his audience in the theatre, be beyond cavil. In this play, Brecht proves himself to be, with Shaw, one of the very few modern playwrights who can compel belief in the greatness of their great ones.

It would be a pity if we were so busy arguing the *Problematik* of science and authority that we overlooked an achievement of this sort. Playwrights, after all, should be allowed their limitations in the stratosphere of science and philosophy, since their main job is down on earth, giving life to characters. The role which, however misleadingly, goes by the name of Galileo Galilei is not only notable in itself, and functions well in the Action, as I have tried to show, it also solves a very real problem posed by Brecht's subject. Our world is no longer in the center of the universe, *ergo* man has lost his central importance in the scheme of things. If this proposition is not of the seventeenth century, it is very much of the twentieth, and it had always been important to Bertolt Brecht. He places it at the heart of Garga's nihilism in *In the Swamp* (*Jungle of Cities*), and of Uriah Shelley's in one of the versions of *A Man's A Man*. Man is absolutely nothing, is Uriah's premise and conclusion. And yet Galileo Galilei, who (allegedly) made this discovery is something? Is this in fact the ultimate contradiction about him? Actually, he is assigned his share in worthlessness and nihilism (if nothingness is divisible), particularly in the later text. But, of course, the main point is in the contrast between this discovery of nothingness and the something-ness, the greatness, of the discoverer. God, as Brecht's Galileo puts it, will be found, from now on, "in ourselves or nowhere." Man will be great, not by the role assigned to him by Another, nor yet by his position in space, but by his own inherent qualities. If *Galileo II* verges on being merely a repudiation of its protagonist, then, as I have already intimated, it carries Brecht's vision of things less completely than *Galileo I*. But even in *Galileo I* the "crime" must be taken very seriously, because it is an abdication of what the protagonist alone has to offer (human greatness), and if human greatness were wiped from the record, then the "discovery" that "man is nothing" would be the truth.

Or are the sterling, but more modest merits of Andrea and Federzoni sufficient to justify existence? In the terms imposed by the play, it is not clear that they are. That these two men disapprove of the abjuration tells us nothing to the purpose. They were never put to such a test. Nor could they be, since, not possessing greatness, they could never have had as much to lose as Galileo had. "The hero is the people." I have conceded that there is much truth in Benjamin's dictum, but the thought in the play is "dialectical," many-sided, ironic, and the individual greatness of the protagonist is essential to the scheme. In the final crisis, he is an anti-hero, and that is bad (or, in the first version, partly bad). What I am stressing, as a final point, is that he is also a hero; the hero as great man; human greatness being what offsets the Copernican blow to human narcissism.

> It was . . . a time which called for giants and produced giants—giants in power of thought, passion, and character, in universality and learning. The men who founded the modern rule of the bourgeoisie had anything but bourgeois limitations. On the contrary the adventurous character of the time inspired them to a greater or less degree. . . . But what is especially characteristic of them is that they almost all pursue their lives and activities in the midst of the contemporary movements, in the practical struggle; they take sides and join in the fight. . . . Hence the fullness and force of character that makes them complete men.

I don't know if this passage from Engels' *Dialectics of Nature* suggested the theme of Galileo Galilei to Brecht. It *is* cited in the Berlin Ensemble program of his play. Reading it, one reflects that, of course, Galileo, according to Brecht, was one who at a crucial moment was disloyal to his "side" in "the fight." That can hardly be unimportant. The character will stand, as Brecht intended, as an exemplar of a certain kind of weakness. But will it not stand, even more impressively, as the exemplar of human greatness, a proof that greatness is possible to humankind? For that matter, would the weakness be even interesting if it were not that of a great (which is to say: in many ways, a strong) man?

—ERIC BENTLEY

GALILEO

It is my opinion that the earth is very noble and admirable by reason of so many and so different alterations and generations which are incessantly made therein.

—GALILEO GALILEI

Characters

GALILEO GALILEI
ANDREA SARTI (*two actors: boy and man*)
MRS. SARTI
LUDOVICO MARSILI
PRIULI, THE CURATOR
SAGREDO, *Galileo's friend*
VIRGINIA GALILEI
TWO SENATORS
MATTI, *an iron founder*
PHILOSOPHER (*later, Rector of the University*)
ELDERLY LADY
YOUNG LADY
FEDERZONI, *assistant to Galileo*
MATHEMATICIAN
LORD CHAMBERLAIN
FAT PRELATE
TWO SCHOLARS
TWO MONKS
INFURIATED MONK
OLD CARDINAL
ATTENDANT MONK
CHRISTOPHER CLAVIUS
FULGANZIO, THE LITTLE MONK
TWO SECRETARIES
CARDINAL BELLARMIN
CARDINAL BARBERINI (*later, Pope Urban VIII*)
CARDINAL INQUISITOR
YOUNG GIRL
HER FRIEND
GIUSEPPE
BALLAD SINGER

HIS WIFE
REVELLER
A LOUD VOICE
INFORMER
TOWN CRIER
OFFICIAL
PEASANT
CUSTOMS OFFICER
BOY
SENATORS, OFFICIALS, PROFESSORS, ARTISANS, LADIES,
    GUESTS, CHILDREN
There are two wordless roles: The DOGE *in Scene 2 and*
PRINCE COSIMO DE' MEDICI *in Scene 4. The ballad of Scene
9 is filled out by a pantomime: among the individuals in
the pantomimic crowd are three extras (including the "*KING
OF HUNGARY*"),* COBBLER'S BOY, THREE CHILDREN, PEAS-
ANT WOMAN, MONK, RICH COUPLE, DWARF, BEGGAR, *and*
GIRL.

SCENE 1

In the year sixteen hundred and nine
Science' light began to shine.
At Padua City, in a modest house,
Galileo Galilei set out to prove
The sun is still, the earth is on the move.

Galileo's scantily furnished study. Morning. GALILEO *is washing himself. A barefooted boy,* ANDREA, *son of his housekeeper,* MRS. SARTI, *enters with a big astronomical model.*

GALILEO: Where did you get that thing?

ANDREA: The coachman brought it.

GALILEO: Who sent it?

ANDREA: It said "From the Court of Naples" on the box.

GALILEO: I don't want their stupid presents. Illuminated manuscripts, a statue of Hercules the size of an elephant—they never send money.

ANDREA: But isn't this an astronomical instrument, Mr. Galilei?

GALILEO: That is an antique too. An expensive toy.

ANDREA: What's it for?

GALILEO: It's a map of the sky according to the wise men of ancient Greece. Bosh! We'll try and sell it to the university. They still teach it there.

ANDREA: How does it work, Mr. Galilei?

GALILEO: It's complicated.

ANDREA: I think I could understand it.

GALILEO (*interested*): Maybe. Let's begin at the beginning. Description!

47

ANDREA: There are metal rings, a lot of them.

GALILEO: How many?

ANDREA: Eight.

GALILEO: Correct. And?

ANDREA: There are words painted on the bands.

GALILEO: What words?

ANDREA: The names of stars.

GALILEO: Such as?

ANDREA: Here is a band with the sun on it and on the inside band is the moon.

GALILEO: Those metal bands represent crystal globes, eight of them.

ANDREA: Crystal?

GALILEO: Like huge soap bubbles one inside the other and the stars are supposed to be tacked onto them. Spin the band with the sun on it. (ANDREA *does so.*) You see the fixed ball in the middle?

ANDREA: Yes.

GALILEO: That's the earth. For two thousand years man has chosen to believe that the sun and all the host of stars revolve about him. Well. The Pope, the cardinals, the princes, the scholars, captains, merchants, house-wives, have pictured themselves squatting in the middle of an affair like that.

ANDREA: Locked up inside?

GALILEO (*triumphant*): Ah!

ANDREA: It's like a cage.

GALILEO: So you sensed that. (*Standing near the model:*) I like to think the ships began it.

ANDREA: Why?

GALILEO: They used to hug the coasts and then all of a sudden they left the coasts and spread over the oceans. A new age was coming. I was onto it years ago. I was a young man, in Siena. There was a group of masons arguing. They had to raise a block of granite.

It was hot. To help matters, one of them wanted to try a new arrangement of ropes. After five minutes' discussion, out went a method which had been employed for a thousand years. The millennium of faith is ended, said I, this is the millennium of doubt. And we are pulling out of that contraption. The sayings of the wise men won't wash any more. Everybody, at last, is getting nosy. I predict that in our time astronomy will become the gossip of the market place and the sons of fishwives will pack the schools.

ANDREA: You're off again, Mr. Galilei. Give me the towel. (*He wipes some soap from Galileo's back.*)

GALILEO: By that time, with any luck, they will be learning that the earth rolls round the sun, and that their mothers, the captains, the scholars, the princes, and the Pope are rolling with it.

ANDREA: That turning-around business is no good. I can see with my own eyes that the sun comes up one place in the morning and goes down in a different place in the evening. It doesn't stand still—I can see it move.

GALILEO: You see nothing, all you do is gawk. Gawking is not seeing. (*He puts the iron washstand in the middle of the room.*) Now—that's the sun. Sit down. (ANDREA *sits on a chair.* GALILEO *stands behind him.*) Where is the sun, on your right or on your left?

ANDREA: Left.

GALILEO: And how will it get to the right?

ANDREA: By your putting it there, of course.

GALILEO: Of course? (*He picks* ANDREA *up, chair and all, and carries him round to the other side of the washstand.*) *Now* where is the sun?

ANDREA: On the right.

GALILEO: And did it move?

ANDREA: I did.

GALILEO: Wrong. Stupid! The chair moved.

ANDREA: But I was on it.

GALILEO: Of course. The chair is the earth, and you're sitting on it.

MRS. SARTI, *who has come in with a glass of milk and a roll, has been watching.*

MRS. SARTI: What are you doing with my son, Mr. Galilei?

ANDREA: Now, mother, you don't understand.

MRS. SARTI: You understand, don't you? Last night he tried to tell me that the earth goes round the sun. You'll soon have him saying that two times two is five.

GALILEO (*eating his breakfast*): Apparently we are on the threshold of a new era, Mrs. Sarti.

MRS. SARTI: Well, I hope we can pay the milkman in this new era. A young gentleman is here to take private lessons and he is well-dressed and don't you frighten him away like you did the others. Wasting your time with Andrea! (*To* ANDREA:) How many times have I told you not to wheedle free lessons out of Mr. Galilei? (*She goes.*)

GALILEO: So you thought enough of the turning-around business to tell your mother about it.

ANDREA: Just to surprise her.

GALILEO: Andrea, I wouldn't talk about our ideas outside.

ANDREA: Why not?

GALILEO: Certain of the authorities won't like it.

ANDREA: Why not, if it's the truth?

GALILEO (*laughs*): Because we are like the worms who are little and have dim eyes and can hardly see the stars at all, and the new astronomy is a framework of guesses or very little more—yet.

MRS. SARTI *shows in* LUDOVICO MARSILI, *a presentable young man.*

GALILEO: This house is like a market place. (*Pointing to*

the model:) Move that out of the way! Put it down there!

LUDOVICO *does so*.

LUDOVICO: Good morning, sir. My name is Ludovico Marsili.

GALILEO (*reading a letter of recommendation he has brought*): You came by way of Holland and your family lives in the Campagna? Private lessons, thirty scudi a month.

LUDOVICO: That's all right, of course, sir.

GALILEO: What is your subject?

LUDOVICO: Horses.

GALILEO: Aha.

LUDOVICO: I don't understand science, sir.

GALILEO: Aha.

LUDOVICO: They showed me an instrument like that in Amsterdam. You'll pardon me, sir, but it didn't make sense to me at all.

GALILEO: It's out of date now.

ANDREA *goes*.

LUDOVICO: You'll have to be patient with me, sir. Nothing in science makes sense to me.

GALILEO: Aha.

LUDOVICO: I saw a brand-new instrument in Amsterdam. A tube affair. "See things five times as large as life!" It had two lenses, one at each end, one lens bulged and the other was like that. (*Gesture.*) Any normal person would think that different lenses cancel each other out. They didn't! I just stood and looked a fool.

GALILEO: I don't quite follow you. What does one see enlarged?

LUDOVICO: Church steeples, pigeons, boats. Anything at a distance.

GALILEO: Did you yourself—see things enlarged?

LUDOVICO: Yes, sir.

GALILEO: And the tube had two lenses? Was it like this? (*He has been making a sketch.*)

LUDOVICO *nods.*

GALILEO: A recent invention?

LUDOVICO: It must be. They only started peddling it on the streets a few days before I left Holland.

GALILEO (*starts to scribble calculations on the sketch; almost friendly*): Why do you bother your head with science? Why don't you just breed horses?

Enter MRS. SARTI. GALILEO *doesn't see her. She listens to the following.*

LUDOVICO: My mother is set on the idea that science is necessary nowadays for conversation.

GALILEO: Aha. You'll find Latin or philosophy easier. (MRS. SARTI *catches his eye.*) I'll see you on Tuesday afternoon.

LUDOVICO: I shall look forward to it, sir.

GALILEO: Good morning. (*He goes to the window and shouts into the street:*) Andrea! Hey, Redhead, Redhead!

MRS. SARTI: The curator of the museum is here to see you.

GALILEO: Don't look at me like that. I took him, didn't I?

MRS. SARTI: I caught your eye in time.

GALILEO: Show the curator in.

She goes. He scribbles something on a new sheet of paper. The CURATOR *comes in.*

CURATOR: Good morning, Mr. Galilei.

GALILEO: Lend me a scudo. (*He takes it and goes to the window, wrapping the coin in the paper on which he has been scribbling.*) Redhead, run to the spectacle-maker and bring me two lenses; here are the measurements. (*He throws the paper out the window. During the following scene* GALILEO *studies his sketch of the lenses.*)

CURATOR: Mr. Galilei, I have come to return your petition for an honorarium. Unfortunately I am unable to recommend your request.

GALILEO: My good sir, how can I make ends meet on five hundred scudi?

CURATOR: What about your private students?

GALILEO: If I spend all my time with students, when am I to study? My particular science is on the threshold of important discoveries. (*He throws a manuscript on the table.*) Here are my findings on the laws of falling bodies. That should be worth two hundred scudi.

CURATOR: I am sure that any paper of yours is of infinite worth, Mr. Galilei. . . .

GALILEO: I was limiting it to two hundred scudi.

CURATOR (*cool*): Mr. Galilei, if you want money and leisure, go to Florence. I have no doubt Prince Cosimo de' Medici will be glad to subsidize you, but eventually you will be forbidden to think—in the name of the Inquisition. (GALILEO *says nothing.*) Now let us not make a mountain out of a molehill. You are happy here in the Republic of Venice but you need money. Well, that's human, Mr. Galilei. May I suggest a simple solution? You remember that chart you made for the army to extract cube roots without any knowledge of mathematics? Now that was practical!

GALILEO: Bosh!

CURATOR: Don't say bosh about something that astounded the Chamber of Commerce. Our city elders are businessmen. Why don't you invent something useful that will bring them a little profit?

GALILEO (*playing with the sketch of the lenses; suddenly*): I see. Mr. Priuli, I may have something for you.

CURATOR: You don't say so.

GALILEO: It's not quite there yet, but . . .

CURATOR: You've never let me down yet, Galilei.

GALILEO: You are always an inspiration to me, Priuli.

CURATOR: You are a great man: a discontented man, but I've always said you are a great man.

GALILEO (*tartly*): My discontent, Priuli, is for the most part with myself. I am forty-six years of age and have achieved nothing which satisfies me.

CURATOR: I won't disturb you any further.

GALILEO: Thank you. Good morning.

CURATOR: Good morning. And thank you.

He goes. GALILEO *sighs.* ANDREA *returns, bringing lenses.*

ANDREA: One scudo was not enough. I had to leave my cap with him before he'd let me take them away.

GALILEO: We'll get it back someday. Give them to me. (*He takes the lenses over to the window, holding them in the relation they would have in a telescope.*)

ANDREA: What are those for?

GALILEO: Something for the Senate. With any luck, they will rake in two hundred scudi. Take a look!

ANDREA: My, things look close! I can read the copper letters on the bell in the Campanile. And the washerwomen by the river, I can see their washboards!

GALILEO: Get out of the way. (*Looking through the lenses himself.*) Aha!

SCENE 2

No one's virtue is complete:
Great Galileo liked to eat.
You will not resent, we hope,
The truth about his telescope.

*The Great Arsenal of Venice, overlooking the harbor full
of ships.* SENATORS *and* OFFICIALS *on one side,* GALILEO,
his daughter VIRGINIA, *and his friend* SAGREDO, *on the other
side. They are dressed in formal, festive clothes.* VIRGINIA
*is fourteen and charming. She carries a velvet cushion on
which lies a brand-new telescope. Behind* GALILEO *are
some* ARTISANS *from the Arsenal. There are onlookers,*
LUDOVICO *among them.*

CURATOR (*announcing*): Senators, Artisans of the Great
    Arsenal of Venice; Mr. Galileo Galilei, professor of
    mathematics at your University of Padua.

GALILEO *steps forward and starts to speak.*

GALILEO: Members of the High Senate! Gentlemen: I have
    great pleasure, as director of this institute, in present-
    ing for your approval and acceptance an entirely new
    instrument originating from this our Great Arsenal
    of the Republic of Venice. As professor of mathe-
    matics at your University of Padua, your obedient
    servant has always counted it his privilege to offer
    you such discoveries and inventions as might prove
    lucrative to the manufacturers and merchants of our
    Venetian Republic. Thus, in all humility, I tender you

55

this, my optical tube, or telescope, constructed, I assure you, on the most scientific and Christian principles, the product of seventeen years' patient research at your University of Padua.

GALILEO *steps back. The* SENATORS *applaud.*

SAGREDO (*aside to* GALILEO): Now you will be able to pay your bills.

GALILEO: Yes. It will make money for them. But you realize that it is more than a money-making gadget? I turned it on the moon last night . . .

CURATOR (*in his best chamber-of-commerce manner*): Gentlemen: Our Republic is to be congratulated not only because this new acquisition will be one more feather in the cap of Venetian culture—(*polite applause*)—not only because our own Mr. Galilei has generously handed this fresh product of his teeming brain entirely over to you, allowing you to manufacture as many of these highly salable articles as you please—(*considerable applause*)—but, Gentlemen of the Senate, has it occurred to you that—with the help of this remarkable new instrument—the battle fleet of the enemy will be visible to us a full two hours before we are visible to him? (*Tremendous applause.*)

GALILEO (*aside to* SAGREDO): We have been held up three generations for lack of a thing like this. I want to go home.

SAGREDO: What about the moon?

GALILEO: Well, for one thing, it doesn't give off its own light.

CURATOR (*continuing his oration*): And now, Your Excellency, and Members of the Senate, Mr. Galilei entreats you to accept the instrument from the hands of his charming daughter Virginia.

Polite applause. He beckons to VIRGINIA, *who steps forward and presents the telescope to the* DOGE.

CURATOR (*during this*): Mr. Galilei gives his invention entirely into your hands, Gentlemen, enjoining you to construct as many of these instruments as you may please.

More applause. The SENATORS *gather round the telescope, examining it, and looking through it.*

GALILEO (*aside to* SAGREDO): Do you know what the Milky Way is made of?

SAGREDO: No.

GALILEO: I do.

CURATOR (*interrupting*): Congratulations, Mr. Galilei. Your extra five hundred scudi a year are safe.

GALILEO: Pardon? What? Of course, the *five hundred* scudi! Yes!

A prosperous man is standing beside the CURATOR.

CURATOR: Mr. Galilei, Mr. Matti of Florence.

MATTI: You're opening new fields, Mr. Galilei. We could do with you at Florence.

CURATOR: Now, Mr. Matti, leave something to us poor Venetians.

MATTI: It is a pity that a great republic has to seek an excuse to pay its great men their right and proper dues.

CURATOR: Even a great man has to have an incentive. (*He joins the* SENATORS *at the telescope.*)

MATTI: I am an iron founder.

GALILEO: Iron founder!

MATTI: With factories at Pisa and Florence. I wanted to talk to you about a machine you designed for a friend of mine in Padua.

GALILEO: I'll put you onto someone to copy it for you, I am not going to have the time. How are things in Florence?

They wander away.

FIRST SENATOR (*peering*): Extraordinary! They're having their lunch on that frigate. Lobsters! I'm hungry!

Laughter.

SECOND SENATOR: Oh, good heavens, look at her! I must tell my wife to stop bathing on the roof. When can I buy one of these things?

Laughter. VIRGINIA *has spotted* LUDOVICO *among the onlookers and drags him to* GALILEO.

VIRGINIA (*to* LUDOVICO): Did I do it nicely?
LUDOVICO: I thought so.
VIRGINIA: Here's Ludovico to congratulate you, father.
LUDOVICO (*embarrassed*): Congratulations, sir.
GALILEO: I improved it.
LUDOVICO: Yes, sir. I am beginning to understand science.

GALILEO *is surrounded.*

VIRGINIA: Isn't father a great man?
LUDOVICO: Yes.
VIRGINIA: Isn't that new thing father made pretty?
LUDOVICO: Yes, a pretty red. Where I saw it first it was covered in green.
VIRGINIA: What was?
LUDOVICO: Never mind. (*A short pause.*) Have you ever been to Holland?

They go. All Venice is congratulating GALILEO, *who wants to go home.*

SCENE 3

January ten, sixteen ten:
Galileo Galilei abolishes heaven.*

Galileo's study at Padua. It is night. GALILEO *and* SAGREDO *at a telescope.*

SAGREDO (*softly*): The edge of the crescent is jagged. All along the dark part, near the shiny crescent, bright particles of light keep coming up, one after the other, and growing larger and merging with the bright crescent.

GALILEO: How do you explain those spots of light?

SAGREDO: It can't be true . . .

GALILEO: It *is* true: they are high mountains.

SAGREDO: On a star?

GALILEO: Yes. The shining particles are mountain peaks catching the first rays of the rising sun while the slopes of the mountains are still dark, and what you see is the sunlight moving down from the peaks into the valleys.

SAGREDO: But this gives the lie to all the astronomy that's been taught for the last two thousand years.

GALILEO: Yes. What you are seeing now has been seen by no other man besides myself.

SAGREDO: But the moon can't be an earth with mountains and valleys like our own any more than the earth can be a star.

GALILEO: The moon *is* an earth with mountains and valleys, and the earth *is* a star. As the moon appears to us,

59

so we appear to the moon. From the moon, the earth looks something like a crescent, sometimes like a half globe, sometimes a full globe, and sometimes it is not visible at all.

SAGREDO: Galileo, this is frightening.

An urgent knocking on the door.

GALILEO: I've discovered something else, something even more astonishing.

More knocking. GALILEO *opens the door and the* CURATOR *comes in.*

CURATOR: There it is—your "miraculous optical tube." Do you know that this invention he so picturesquely termed "the fruit of seventeen years' research" will be on sale tomorrow for two scudi apiece at every street corner in Venice? A shipload of them has just arrived from Holland.

SAGREDO: Oh, dear!

GALILEO *turns his back and adjusts the telescope.*

CURATOR: When I think of the poor gentlemen of the Senate who believed they were getting an invention they could monopolize for their own profit. . . . Why, when they took their first look through the glass, it was only by the merest chance that they didn't see a peddler, seven times enlarged, selling tubes exactly like it at the corner of the street.

SAGREDO: Mr. Priuli, with the help of this instrument, Mr. Galilei has made discoveries that will revolutionize our concept of the universe.

CURATOR: Mr. Galilei provided the city with a first-rate water pump and the irrigation works he designed function splendidly. How was I to expect this?

GALILEO (*still at the telescope*): Not so fast, Priuli. I may be on the track of a very large gadget. Certain of the stars appear to have regular movements. If there were a clock in the sky, it could be seen from anywhere. That might be useful for your shipowners.

CURATOR: I won't listen to you. I listened to you before, and as a reward for my friendship you have made me the laughingstock of the town. You can laugh—you got your money. But let me tell you this: you've destroyed my faith in a lot of things, Mr. Galilei. I'm disgusted with the world. That's all I have to say. (*He storms out.*)

GALILEO (*embarrassed*): Businessmen bore me, they suffer so. Did you see the frightened look in his eyes when he caught sight of a world not created solely for the purpose of doing business?

SAGREDO: Did you know that telescopes had been made in Holland?

GALILEO: I'd heard about it. But the one I made for the Senators was twice as good as any Dutchman's. Besides, I needed the money. How can I work, with the tax collector on the doorstep? And my poor daughter will never acquire a husband unless she has a dowry, she's not too bright. And I like to buy books—all kinds of books. Why not? And what about my appetite? I don't think well unless I eat well. Can I help it if I get my best ideas over a good meal and a bottle of wine? They don't pay me as much as they pay the butcher's boy. If only I could have five years to do nothing but research! Come on. I am going to show you something else.

SAGREDO: I don't know that I want to look again.

GALILEO: This is one of the brighter nebulae of the Milky Way. What do you see?

SAGREDO: But it's made up of stars—countless stars.

GALILEO: Countless worlds.

SAGREDO (*hesitating*): What about the theory that the earth revolves round the sun? Have you run across anything about that?

GALILEO: No. But I noticed something on Tuesday that might prove a step towards even that. Where's Jupiter? There are four lesser stars near Jupiter. I happened on them on Monday but didn't take any particular note of their position. On Tuesday I looked again. I could have sworn they had moved. They have changed again. Tell me what you see.

SAGREDO: I only see three.

GALILEO: Where's the fourth? Let's get the charts and settle down to work.

They work and the lights dim. The lights go up again. It is near dawn.

GALILEO: The only place the fourth can be is round at the back of the larger star where we cannot see it. This means there are small stars revolving around a big star. Where are the crystal shells now, that the stars are supposed to be fixed to?

SAGREDO: Jupiter can't be attached to anything: there are other stars revolving round it.

GALILEO: There is no support in the heavens. (SAGREDO *laughs awkwardly*.) Don't stand there looking at me as if it weren't true.

SAGREDO: I suppose it is true. I'm afraid.

GALILEO: Why?

SAGREDO: What do you think is going to happen to you for saying that there is another sun around which other earths revolve? And that there are only stars and no difference between earth and heaven? Where is God then?

GALILEO: What do you mean?

SAGREDO: God? Where is God?

GALILEO (*angrily*): Not there! Any more than He'd be here—if creatures from the moon came down to look for Him!

SAGREDO: Then where is He?

GALILEO: I'm not a theologian: I'm a mathematician.

SAGREDO: You are a human being! (*Almost shouting:*) Where is God in your system of the universe?

GALILEO: Within ourselves. Or—nowhere.

SAGREDO: Ten years ago a man was burned at the stake for saying that.

GALILEO: Giordano Bruno was an idiot: he spoke too soon. He would never have been condemned if he could have backed up what he said with proof.

SAGREDO (*incredulously*): Do you really believe proof will make any difference?

GALILEO: I believe in the human race. The only people that can't be reasoned with are the dead. Human beings are intelligent.

SAGREDO: Intelligent—or merely shrewd?

GALILEO: I know they call a donkey a horse when they want to sell it, and a horse a donkey when they want to buy it. But is that the whole story? Aren't they susceptible to truth as well? (*He fishes a small pebble out of his pocket.*) If anybody were to drop a stone—(*drops the pebble*)—and tell them that it didn't fall, do you think they would keep quiet? The evidence of your own eyes is a very seductive thing. Sooner or later everybody must succumb to it.

SAGREDO: Galileo, I am helpless when you talk.

A church bell has been ringing for some time, calling people to mass. Enter VIRGINIA, *muffled up for mass, carrying a candle, protected from the wind by a globe.*

VIRGINIA: Oh, father, you promised to go to bed tonight, and it's five o'clock again.

GALILEO: Why are you up at this hour?

VIRGINIA: I'm going to mass with Mrs. Sarti. Ludovico is going too. How was the night, father?

GALILEO: Bright.

VIRGINIA: What did you find through the tube?

GALILEO: Only some little specks by the side of a star. I must draw attention to them somehow. I think I'll name them after the Prince of Florence. Why not call them the Medicean planets? By the way, we may move to Florence. I've written to His Highness, asking if he can use me as Court Mathematician.

VIRGINIA: Oh, father, we'll be at the court!

SAGREDO (*amazed*): Galileo!

GALILEO: My dear Sagredo, I must have leisure. My only worry is that His Highness after all may not take me. I'm not accustomed to writing formal letters to great personages. Here, do you think this is the right sort of thing?

SAGREDO (*reads*): "Whose sole desire is to reside in Your Highness' presence—the rising sun of our great age." Cosimo de' Medici is a boy of nine.

GALILEO: The only way a man like me can land a good job is by crawling on his stomach. Your father, my dear, is going to take his share of the pleasures of life in exchange for all his hard work, and about time too. I have no patience, Sagredo, with a man who doesn't use his brains to fill his belly. Run along to mass now.

VIRGINIA *goes.*

SAGREDO: Galileo, do not go to Florence.

GALILEO: Why not?

SAGREDO: The monks are in power there.

GALILEO: Going to mass is a small price to pay for a full belly. And there are many famous scholars at the court of Florence.

SAGREDO: Court monkeys.

GALILEO: I shall enjoy taking them by the scruff of the neck and making them look through the telescope.

SAGREDO: Galileo, you are traveling the road to disaster. You are suspicious and skeptical in science, but in politics you are as naïve as your daughter! How can people in power leave a man at large who tells the truth, even if it be the truth about the distant stars? Can you see the Pope scribbling a note in his diary: "Tenth of January, 1610, Heaven abolished"? A moment ago, when you were at the telescope, I saw you tied to the stake, and when you said you believed in proof, I smelt burning flesh!

GALILEO: I am going to Florence.

Before the next scene, a curtain with the following legend on it is lowered:

> BY SETTING THE NAME OF MEDICI IN THE SKY, I AM BESTOWING IMMORTALITY UPON THE STARS. I COMMEND MYSELF TO YOU AS YOUR MOST FAITHFUL AND DEVOTED SERVANT, WHOSE SOLE DESIRE IS TO RESIDE IN YOUR HIGHNESS' PRESENCE, THE RISING SUN OF OUR GREAT AGE.
>
> —GALILEO GALILEI

SCENE 4

Galileo's house at Florence. Well-appointed. GALILEO *is demonstrating his telescope to* PRINCE COSIMO DE' MEDICI, *a boy of nine, accompanied by his* LORD CHAMBERLAIN, LADIES *and* GENTLEMEN *of the court, and an assortment of university* PROFESSORS. *With* GALILEO *are* ANDREA *and* FEDERZONI, *the new assistant (an old man).* MRS. SARTI *stands by. Before the scene opens, the voice of the* PHILOSOPHER *can be heard.*

VOICE OF THE PHILOSOPHER: Quaedam miracula universi. Orbes mystice canorae, arcus crystallini, circulatio corporum coelestium. Cyclorum epicyclorumque intoxicatio, integritas tabulae chordarum et architectura elata globorum coelestium.

GALILEO: Shall we speak in everyday language? My colleague Mr. Federzoni does not understand Latin.

PHILOSOPHER: Is it necessary that he should?

GALILEO: Yes.

PHILOSOPHER: Forgive me. I thought he was your mechanic.

ANDREA: Mr. Federzoni is a mechanic and a scholar.

PHILOSOPHER: Thank you, young man. If Mr. Federzoni insists . . .

GALILEO: I insist.

PHILOSOPHER: It will not be as clear, but it's your house. Your Highness . . . (*The* PRINCE *is ineffectually trying to establish contact with* ANDREA.) I was about to recall to Mr. Galilei some of the wonders of the universe as they are set down for us in the Divine Classics. (*The* LADIES *"ah."*) Remind him of the "mystically musical spheres, the crystal arches, the circulation of the heavenly bodies—"

66

ELDERLY LADY: Perfect poise!

PHILOSOPHER: "—the intoxication of the cycles and epicycles, the integrity of the tables of chords, and the enraptured architecture of the celestial globes."

ELDERLY LADY: What diction!

PHILOSOPHER: May I pose the question: Why should we go out of our way to look for things that can only strike a discord in the ineffable harmony?

The LADIES *applaud.*

FEDERZONI: Take a look through here—you'll be interested.

ANDREA: Sit down here, please.

The PROFESSORS *laugh.*

MATHEMATICIAN: Mr. Galilei, nobody doubts that your brain child—or is it your adopted brain child?—is brilliantly contrived.

GALILEO: Your Highness, one can see the four stars as large as life, you know.

The PRINCE *looks to the* ELDERLY LADY *for guidance.*

MATHEMATICIAN: Ah. But has it occurred to you that an eyeglass through which one sees such phenomena might not be a too reliable eyeglass?

GALILEO: How is that?

MATHEMATICIAN: If one could be sure you would keep your temper, Mr. Galilei, I could suggest that what one sees in the eyeglass and what is in the heavens are two entirely different things.

GALILEO (*quietly*): You are suggesting fraud?

MATHEMATICIAN: No! How could I, in the presence of His Highness?

ELDERLY LADY: The gentlemen are just wondering if Your Highness' stars are really, really there!

Pause.

YOUNG LADY (*trying to be helpful*): Can one see the claws on the Great Bear?

GALILEO: And everything on Taurus the Bull.

FEDERZONI: Are you going to look through it or not?

MATHEMATICIAN: With the greatest of pleasure.

> *Pause. Nobody goes near the telescope. All of a sudden the boy* ANDREA *turns and marches pale and erect past them through the whole length of the room. The* GUESTS *follow with their eyes.*

MRS. SARTI (*as he passes her*): What is the matter with you?

ANDREA (*shocked*): They are wicked.

PHILOSOPHER: Your Highness, it is a delicate matter and I had no intention of bringing it up, but Mr. Galilei was about to demonstrate the impossible. His new stars would have broken the outer crystal sphere—which we know of on the authority of Aristotle. I am sorry.

MATHEMATICIAN: The last word.

FEDERZONI: He had no telescope.

MATHEMATICIAN: Quite.

GALILEO (*keeping his temper*): "Truth is the daughter of Time, not of Authority." Gentlemen, the sum of our knowledge is pitiful. It has been my singular good fortune to find a new instrument which brings a small patch of the universe a little bit closer. It is at your disposal.

PHILOSOPHER: Where is all this leading?

GALILEO: Are we, as scholars, concerned with where the truth might lead us?

PHILOSOPHER: Mr. Galilei, the truth might lead us anywhere!

GALILEO: I can only beg you to look through my eyeglass.

MATHEMATICIAN (*wild*): If I understand Mr. Galilei correctly, he is asking us to discard the teachings of two thousand years.

GALILEO: For two thousand years we have been looking at the sky and didn't see the four moons of Jupiter, and there they were all the time. Why defend shaken teachings? You should be doing the shaking. (*The* PRINCE *is sleepy.*) Your Highness! My work in the Great Arsenal of Venice brought me in daily contact with sailors, carpenters, and so on. These men are unread. They depend on the evidence of their senses. But they taught me many new ways of doing things. The question is whether these gentlemen here want to be found out as fools by men who might not have had the advantages of a classical education but who are not afraid to use their eyes. I tell you that our dockyards are stirring with that same high curiosity which was the true glory of ancient Greece.

Pause.

PHILOSOPHER: I have no doubt Mr. Galilei's theories will arouse the enthusiasm of the dockyards.

CHAMBERLAIN: Your Highness, I find to my amazement that this highly informative discussion has exceeded the time we had allowed for it. May I remind Your Highness that the State Ball begins in three-quarters of an hour?

The COURT *bows low.*

ELDERLY LADY: We would really have liked to look through your eyeglass, Mr. Galilei, wouldn't we, Your Highness?

The PRINCE *bows politely and is led to the door.* GALILEO *follows the* PRINCE, CHAMBERLAIN, *and* LADIES *toward the exit. The* PROFESSORS *remain at the telescope.*

GALILEO (*almost servile*): All anybody has to do is look through the telescope, Your Highness.

MRS. SARTI *takes a plate with candies to the* PRINCE *as he is walking out.*

MRS. SARTI: A piece of homemade candy, Your Highness?

ELDERLY LADY: Not now. Thank you. It is too soon before His Highness' supper.

PHILOSOPHER: Wouldn't I like to take that thing to pieces.

MATHEMATICIAN: Ingenious contraption. It must be quite difficult to keep clean. (*He rubs the lens with his handkerchief and looks at the handkerchief.*)

FEDERZONI: We did not paint the Medicean stars on the lens.

ELDERLY LADY (*to the* PRINCE, *who has whispered something to her*): No, no, no, there is nothing the matter with your stars!

CHAMBERLAIN (*across the stage to* GALILEO): His Highness will of course seek the opinion of the greatest living authority: Christopher Clavius, Chief Astronomer to the Papal College in Rome.

SCENE 5

Things take indeed a wondrous turn
When learned men do stoop to learn.
Clavius, we are pleased to say,
Upheld Galileo Galilei.

A burst of laughter is heard and the curtains reveal a hall in the Collegium Romanum. HIGH CHURCHMEN, MONKS, *and* SCHOLARS *standing about talking and laughing.* GALILEO *by himself in a corner.*

FAT PRELATE (*shaking with laughter*): Hopeless! Hopeless! Hopeless! Will you tell me something people won't believe?

A SCHOLAR: Yes, that you don't love your stomach!

FAT PRELATE: They'd believe that. They only do not believe what's good for them. They doubt the devil, but fill them up with some fiddle-de-dee about the earth rolling like a marble in the gutter and they swallow it hook, line, and sinker. Sancta simplicitas!

He laughs until the tears run down his cheeks. The others laugh with him. A group has formed whose members boisterously begin to pretend they are standing on a rolling globe.

A MONK: It's rolling fast, I'm dizzy. May I hold onto you, Professor? (*He sways dizzily and clings to one of the scholars for support.*)

THE SCHOLAR: Old Mother Earth's been at the bottle again. Whoa!

71

MONK: Hey! Hey! We're slipping off! Help!

SECOND SCHOLAR: Look! There's Venus! Hold me, lads. Whee!

SECOND MONK: Don't, don't hurl us off onto the moon. There are nasty sharp mountain peaks on the moon, brethren!

VARIOUSLY: Hold tight! Hold tight! Don't look down! Hold tight! It'll make you giddy!

FAT PRELATE: And we cannot have giddy people in Holy Rome.

They rock with laughter. An INFURIATED MONK *comes out from a large door at the rear holding a Bible in his hand and pointing out a page with his finger.*

INFURIATED MONK: What does the Bible say—"Sun, stand thou still on Gideon and thou, moon, in the valley of Ajalon." Can the sun come to a standstill if it doesn't ever move? Does the Bible lie?

FAT PRELATE: How did Christopher Clavius, the greatest astronomer we have, get mixed up in an investigation of this kind?

INFURIATED MONK: He's in there with his eye glued to that diabolical instrument.

FAT PRELATE (*to* GALILEO, *who has been playing with his pebble and has dropped it*): Mr. Galilei, something dropped down.

GALILEO: Monsignor, are you sure it didn't drop up?

INFURIATED MONK: As astronomers we are aware that there are phenomena which are beyond us, but man can't expect to understand everything!

Enter a very old CARDINAL *leaning on a* MONK *for support. Others move aside.*

OLD CARDINAL: Aren't they out yet? Can't they reach a decision on that paltry matter? Christopher Clavius ought to know his astronomy after all these years. I

am informed that Mr. Galilei transfers mankind from
the center of the universe to somewhere on the out-
skirts. Mr. Galilei is therefore an enemy of mankind
and must be dealt with as such. Is it conceivable that
God would trust this most precious fruit of His labor
to a minor, frolicking star? Would He have sent His
Son to such a place? How can there be people with
such twisted minds that they believe what they're
told by the slave of a multiplication table?

FAT PRELATE (*quietly to* CARDINAL): The gentleman is
over there.

OLD CARDINAL: So you are the man. You know my eyes
are not what they were, but I can see you bear a
striking resemblance to the man we burned. What
was his name?

MONK: Your Eminence must avoid excitement the doctor
said . . .

OLD CARDINAL (*disregarding him*): So you have degraded
the earth despite the fact that you live by her and
receive everything from her. I won't have it! I won't
have it! I won't be a nobody on an inconsequential
star briefly twirling hither and thither. I tread the
earth, and the earth is firm beneath my feet, and
there is no motion to the earth, and the earth is the
center of all things, and I am the center of the earth,
and the eye of the Creator is upon me. About me
revolve, affixed to their crystal shells, the lesser lights
of the stars and the great light of the sun, created
to give light upon me that God might see me—Man,
God's greatest effort, the center of creation. "In the
image of God created He him." Immortal . . . (*His
strength fails him and he catches for the* MONK *for
support.*)

MONK: You mustn't overtax your strength, Your Eminence.

At this moment the door at the rear opens and
CHRISTOPHER CLAVIUS *enters followed by his* AS-

TRONOMERS. *He strides hastily across the hall, looking neither to right nor left. As he goes by we hear him say—*

CLAVIUS: He is right.

Deadly silence. All turn to GALILEO.

OLD CARDINAL: What is it? Have they reached a decision?

No one speaks.

MONK: It is time that Your Eminence went home.

The hall is emptying fast. One little MONK *who had entered with* CLAVIUS *speaks to* GALILEO.

LITTLE MONK: Mr. Galilei, I heard Father Clavius say: "Now it's for the theologians to set the heavens right again." You have won.

Before the next scene, a curtain with the following legend on it is lowered:

AS THESE NEW ASTRONOMICAL CHARTS ENABLE US TO DETERMINE LONGITUDES AT SEA AND SO MAKE IT POSSIBLE TO REACH THE NEW CONTINENTS BY THE SHORTEST ROUTES, WE WOULD BESEECH YOUR EXCELLENCY TO AID US IN REACHING MR. GALILEI, MATHEMATICIAN TO THE COURT OF FLORENCE, WHO IS NOW IN ROME . . .
> —FROM A LETTER WRITTEN BY A MEMBER OF THE GENOA CHAMBER OF COMMERCE AND NAVIGATION TO THE PAPAL LEGATION.

SCENE 6

When Galileo was in Rome
A Cardinal asked him to his home.
He wined and dined him as his guest
And only made one small request.

Cardinal Bellarmin's house in Rome. Music is heard and the chatter of many guests. Two SECRETARIES *are at the rear of the stage at a desk.* GALILEO, *his daughter* VIRGINIA, *now twenty-one, and* LUDOVICO MARSILI, *who has become her fiancé, are just arriving. A few* GUESTS, *standing near the entrance with masks in their hands, nudge each other and are suddenly silent.* GALILEO *looks at them. They applaud him politely and bow.*

VIRGINIA: Oh, father! I'm so happy. I won't dance with anyone but you, Ludovico.

GALILEO (*to a* SECRETARY): I was to wait here for His Eminence.

FIRST SECRETARY: His Eminence will be with you in a few minutes.

VIRGINIA: Do I look proper?

LUDOVICO: You are showing some lace.

GALILEO *puts his arms around their shoulders.*

GALILEO (*quoting mischievously*):

> Fret not, daughter, if perchance
> You attract a wanton glance.
> The eyes that catch a trembling lace

75

> Will guess the heartbeat's quickened pace.
> Lovely woman still may be
> Careless with felicity.

VIRGINIA (*to* GALILEO): Feel my heart.
GALILEO (*to* LUDOVICO): It's thumping.
VIRGINIA: I hope I always say the right thing.
LUDOVICO: She's afraid she's going to let us down.
VIRGINIA: Oh, I want to look beautiful.
GALILEO: You'd better. If you don't they'll start saying all over again that the earth doesn't turn.
LUDOVICO (*laughing*): It *doesn't* turn, sir.

GALILEO *laughs.*

GALILEO: Go and enjoy yourselves. (*He speaks to one of the* SECRETARIES:) A large fete?
FIRST SECRETARY: Two hundred and fifty guests, Mr. Galilei. We have represented here this evening most of the great families of Italy, the Orsinis, the Villanis, the Nuccolis, the Soldanieris, the Canes, the Lecchis, the Estes, the Colombinis, the . . .

VIRGINIA *comes running back.*

VIRGINIA: Oh, father, I didn't tell you: you're famous.
GALILEO: Why?
VIRGINIA: The hairdresser in the Via Vittorio kept four other ladies waiting and took me first. (*Exit.*)
GALILEO (*at the stairway, leaning over the well*): Rome!

Enter CARDINAL BELLARMIN, *wearing the mask of a lamb, and* CARDINAL BARBERINI, *wearing the mask of a dove.*

SECRETARIES: Their Eminences, Cardinals Bellarmin and Barberini.

The CARDINALS *lower their masks.*

GALILEO (*to* BELLARMIN): Your Eminence.

BELLARMIN: Mr. Galilei, Cardinal Barberini.

GALILEO: Your Eminence.

BARBERINI: So you are the father of that lovely child!

BELLARMIN: Who is inordinately proud of being her father's daughter.

They laugh.

BARBERINI (*points his finger at* GALILEO): "The sun riseth and setteth and returneth to its place," saith the Bible. What saith Galilei?

GALILEO: Appearances are notoriously deceptive, Your Eminence. Once, when I was so high, I was standing on a ship that was pulling away from the shore and I shouted, "The shore is moving!" I know now that it was the ship which was moving.

BARBERINI (*laughs*): You can't catch that man. I tell you, Bellarmin, his moons around Jupiter are hard nuts to crack. Unfortunately for me I happened to glance at a few papers on astronomy once. It is harder to get rid of than the itch.

BELLARMIN: Let's move with the times. If it makes navigation easier for sailors to use new charts based on a new hypothesis, let them have them. We only have to scotch doctrines that contradict Holy Writ.

He leans over the balustrade of the well and acknowledges various GUESTS.

BARBERINI: But Bellarmin, you haven't caught onto this fellow. The scriptures don't satisfy him. Copernicus does.

GALILEO: Copernicus? "He that withholdeth corn, the people shall curse him." Book of Proverbs.

BARBERINI: "A prudent man concealeth knowledge." Also Book of Proverbs.

GALILEO: "Where no oxen are, the crib is clean: but much increase is by the strength of the ox."

BARBERINI: "He that ruleth his spirit is better than he that taketh a city."

GALILEO: "But a broken spirit drieth the bones." (*Pause.*) "Doth not wisdom cry?"

BARBERINI: "Can one go upon hot coals and his feet not be burned?" Welcome to Rome, friend Galileo. You recall the legend of our city's origin? Two small boys found sustenance and refuge with a she-wolf and from that day we have paid the price for the she-wolf's milk. But the place is not bad. We have everything for your pleasure—from a scholarly dispute with Bellarmin to ladies of high degree. Look at that woman flaunting herself. No? He wants a weighty discussion! All right! (*To* GALILEO:) You people speak in terms of circles and ellipses and regular velocities—simple movements that the human mind can grasp—very convenient—but suppose Almighty God had taken it into His head to make the stars move like that—(*he describes an irregular motion with his fingers through the air*)—then where would you be?

GALILEO: My good man—the Almighty would have endowed us with brains like that—(*repeats the movement*)—so that we could grasp the movements—(*repeats the movement*)—like that. I believe in the brain.

BARBERINI: I consider the brain inadequate. He doesn't answer. He is too polite to tell me he considers *my* brain inadequate. What is one to do with him? Butter wouldn't melt in his moutl. All he wants to do is to prove that God made a few boners in astronomy. God didn't study His astronomy hard enough before He composed Holy Writ. (*To the* SECRETARIES:)

Don't take anything down. This is a scientific discussion among friends.

BELLARMIN (*to* GALILEO): Does it not appear more probable—even to you—that the Creator knows more about His work than the created?

GALILEO: In his blindness man is liable to misread not only the sky but also the Bible.

BELLARMIN: The interpretation of the Bible is a matter for the ministers of God. (GALILEO *remains silent.*) At last you are quiet. (*He gestures to the* SECRETARIES. *They start writing.*) Tonight the Holy Office has decided that the theory according to which the earth goes around the sun is foolish, absurd, and a heresy. I am charged, Mr. Galilei, with cautioning you to abandon these teachings. (*To the* FIRST SECRETARY:) Would you repeat that?

FIRST SECRETARY (*reading*): "His Eminence, Cardinal Bellarmin, to the aforesaid Galilei: 'The Holy Office has resolved that the theory according to which the earth goes around the sun is foolish, absurd, and a heresy. I am charged, Mr. Galilei, with cautioning you to abandon these teachings.' "

GALILEO (*rocking on his base*): But the facts!

BARBERINI (*consoling*): Your findings have been ratified by the Papal Observatory, Galilei. That should be most flattering to you . . .

BELLARMIN (*cutting in*): The Holy Office formulated the decree without going into details.

GALILEO (*to* BARBERINI): Do you realize, the future of all scientific research is—

BELLARMIN (*cutting in*)· Completely assured, Mr. Galilei. It is not given to man to know the truth: it is granted to him to seek after the truth. Science is the legitimate and beloved daughter of the Church. She must have confidence in the Church.

GALILEO (*infuriated*): I would not try confidence by whistling her too often.

BARBERINI (*quickly*): Be careful what you're doing— you'll be throwing out the baby with the bath water, friend Galilei. (*Serious*:) We need you more than you need us.

BELLARMIN: Well, it is time we introduced our distinguished friend to our guests. The whole country talks of him!

BARBERINI: Let us replace our masks, Bellarmin. Poor Galilei hasn't got one. (*He laughs.*)

They take GALILEO *out.*

FIRST SECRETARY: Did you get his last sentence?

SECOND SECRETARY: Yes. Do you have what he said about believing in the brain?

Another cardinal—the INQUISITOR—*enters.*

INQUISITOR: Did the conference take place?

The FIRST SECRETARY *hands him the papers and the* INQUISITOR *dismisses the* SECRETARIES. *They go. The* INQUISITOR *sits down and starts to read the transcription. Two or three* YOUNG LADIES *skitter across the stage; they see the* INQUISITOR *and curtsy as they go.*

YOUNG GIRL: Who was that?

HER FRIEND: The Cardinal Inquisitor.

They giggle and go. Enter VIRGINIA. *She curtsies as she goes. The* INQUISITOR *stops her.*

INQUISITOR: Good evening, my child. Beautiful night. May I congratulate you on your betrothal? Your young man comes from a fine family. Are you staying with us here in Rome?

VIRGINIA: Not now, Your Eminence. I must go home to prepare for the wedding.

INQUISITOR: Ah. You are accompanying your father to Florence. That should please him. Science must be cold comfort in a home. Your youth and warmth will keep him down to earth. It is easy to get lost up there. (*He gestures to the sky.*)

VIRGINIA: He doesn't talk to me about the stars, Your Eminence.

INQUISITOR: No. (*He laughs.*) They don't eat fish in the fisherman's house. I can tell you something about astronomy. My child, it seems that God has blessed our modern astronomers with imaginations. It is quite alarming! Do you know that the earth—which we old fogies supposed to be so large—has shrunk to something no bigger than a walnut, and the new universe has grown so vast that prelates—and even cardinals—look like ants. Why, God Almighty might lose sight of a Pope! I wonder if I know your Father Confessor.

VIRGINIA: Father Christopherus, from Saint Ursula's at Florence, Your Eminence.

INQUISITOR: My dear child, your father will need you. Not so much now perhaps, but one of these days. You are pure, and there is strength in purity. Greatness is sometimes, indeed often, too heavy a burden for those to whom God has granted it. What man is so great that he has no place in a prayer? But I am keeping you, my dear. Your fiancé will be jealous of me, and I am afraid your father will never forgive me for holding forth on astronomy. Go to your dancing and remember me to Father Christopherus.

VIRGINIA *kisses his ring and runs off. The* INQUISITOR *resumes his reading.*

SCENE 7

Galileo, feeling grim,
A young monk came to visit him.
The monk was born of common folk.
It was of science that they spoke.

Garden of the Florentine Ambassador in Rome. Distant
hum of a great city. GALILEO *and the* LITTLE MONK *of*
Scene 5 are talking.

GALILEO: Let's hear it. That robe you're wearing gives
you the right to say whatever you want to say. Let's
hear it.

LITTLE MONK: I have studied physics, Mr. Galilei.

GALILEO: That might help us if it enabled you to admit
that two and two are four.

LITTLE MONK: Mr. Galilei, I have spent four sleepless
nights trying to reconcile the decree that I have read
with the moons of Jupiter that I have seen. This
morning I decided to come to see you after I had
said mass.

GALILEO: To tell me that Jupiter has no moons?

LITTLE MONK: No, I found out that I think the decree a
wise decree. It has shocked me into realizing that free
research has its dangers. I have had to decide to give
up astronomy. However, I felt the impulse to confide
in you some of the motives which have impelled even
a passionate physicist to abandon his work.

GALILEO: Your motives are familiar to me.

LITTLE MONK: You mean, of course, the special powers

invested in certain commissions of the Holy Office? But there is something else I would like to talk to you about my family. I do not come from the great city. My parents are peasants in the Campagna, who know about the cultivation of the olive tree, and not much about anything else. Too often these days when I am trying to concentrate on tracking down the moons of Jupiter, I see my parents. I see them sitting by the fire with my sister, eating their curded cheese. I see the beams of the ceiling above them, which the smoke of centuries has blackened, and I can see the veins stand out on their toil-worn hands, and the little spoons in their hands. They scrape a living, and underlying their poverty there is a sort of order. There are routines. The routine of scrubbing the floors, the routine of the seasons in the olive orchard, the routine of paying taxes. The troubles that come to them are recurrent troubles. My father did not get his poor bent back all at once, but little by little, year by year, in the olive orchard; just as year after year, with unfailing regularity, childbirth has made my mother more and more sexless. They draw the strength they need to sweat with their loaded baskets up the stony paths, to bear children, even to eat, from the sight of the trees greening each year anew, from the reproachful face of the soil, which is never satisfied, and from the little church and Bible texts they hear there on Sunday. They have been told that God relies upon them and that the pageant of the world has been written around them that they may be tested in the important or unimportant parts handed out to them. How could they take it, were I to tell them that they are on a lump of stone ceaselessly spinning in empty space, circling around a second-rate star? What, then, would be the use of their patience, their acceptance of misery? What comfort, then, the Holy Scriptures, which have mercifully explained their crucifixion? The Holy Scriptures would then be proved full of mistakes. No, I see them begin to look frightened. I see them slowly put their spoons down on the table. They would feel cheated. "There is no eye watching over us, after all," they would say. "We have to start out on our own, at our time of life. Nobody has planned a part for us beyond this wretched one on a worthless star. There is no meaning in our misery. Hunger is just not having eaten. It is no test of strength. Effort is just stooping and carrying. It is not a virtue." Can you understand that I read into the decree of the Holy Office a noble, motherly pity and a great goodness of the soul?

GALILEO (*embarrassed*): Hm, well at least you have found out that it is not a question of the satellites of Jupiter, but of the peasants of the Campagna! And don't try to break me down by the halo of beauty that radiates from old age. How does a pearl develop in an oyster? A jagged grain of sand makes its way into the oyster's shell and makes its life unbearable. The oyster exudes slime to cover the grain of sand and the slime eventually hardens into a pearl. The oyster nearly dies in the process. To hell with the pearl, give me the healthy oyster! And virtues are not exclusive to misery. If your parents were prosperous and happy, they might develop the virtues of happiness and prosperity. Today the virtues of exhaustion are caused by the exhausted land. For that, my new water pumps could work more wonders than their ridiculous superhuman efforts. Be fruitful and multiply: for war will cut down the population, and our fields are barren! (*A pause.*) Shall I lie to your people?

LITTLE MONK: We must be silent from the highest of motives: the inward peace of less fortunate souls.

GALILEO: My dear man, as a bonus for not meddling with

your parents' peace, the authorities are tendering me, on a silver platter, persecution-free, my share of the fat sweated from your parents, who, as you know, were made in God's image. Should I condone this decree, my motives might not be disinterested: easy life, no persecution and so on.

LITTLE MONK: Mr. Galilei, I am a priest.

GALILEO: You are also a physicist. How can new machinery be evolved to domesticate the river water if we physicists are forbidden to study, discuss, and pool our findings about the greatest machinery of all, the machinery of the heavenly bodies? Can I reconcile my findings on the paths of falling bodies with the current belief in the tracks of witches on broomsticks? (*A pause.*) I am sorry—I shouldn't have said that.

LITTLE MONK: You don't think that the truth, if it is the truth, would make its way without us?

GALILEO: No! No! No! As much of the truth gets through as we push through. You talk about the Campagna peasants as if they were the moss on their huts. Naturally, if they don't get a move on and learn to think for themselves, the most efficient of irrigation systems cannot help them. I can see their divine patience, but where is their divine fury?

LITTLE MONK (*helpless*): They are old!

GALILEO *stands for a moment, beaten; he cannot meet the Little Monk's eyes. He takes a manuscript from the table and throws it violently on the ground.*

LITTLE MONK: What is that?

GALILEO: Here is writ what draws the ocean when it ebbs and flows. Let it lie there. Thou shalt not read. (*The* LITTLE MONK *has picked up the manuscript.*) Already! An apple of the tree of knowledge, he can't wait, he wolfs it down. He will rot in hell for all eternity. Look at him, where are his manners? Sometimes I think I would let them imprison me in a place a thousand feet beneath the earth, where no light could reach me, if in exchange I could find out what stuff that is: "Light." The bad thing is that, when I find something, I have to boast about it like a lover or a drunkard or a traitor. That is a hopeless vice and leads to the abyss. I wonder how long I shall be content to discuss it with my dog!

LITTLE MONK (*immersed in the manuscript*): I don't understand this sentence.

GALILEO: I'll explain it to you, I'll explain it to you.

They are sitting on the floor.

SCENE 8

Eight long years with tongue in cheek
Of what he knew he did not speak.
Then temptation grew too great
And Galileo challenged fate.

Galileo's house in Florence again. GALILEO *is supervising his assistants*—ANDREA, FEDERZONI, *and the* LITTLE MONK —*who are about to prepare an experiment.* MRS. SARTI *and* VIRGINIA *are at a long table sewing bridal linen. There is a new telescope, larger than the old one. At the moment it is covered with a cloth.*

ANDREA (*looking up a schedule*): Thursday. Afternoon. Floating bodies again. Ice, bowl of water, scales, and it says here an iron needle. Aristotle.
VIRGINIA: Ludovico likes to entertain. We must take care to be neat. His mother notices every stitch. She doesn't approve of father's books.
MRS. SARTI: That's all a thing of the past. He hasn't published a book for years.
VIRGINIA: That's true. Oh, Sarti, it's fun sewing a trousseau.
MRS. SARTI: Virginia, I want to talk to you. You are very young, and you have no mother, and your father is putting those pieces of ice in water, and marriage is too serious a business to go into blind. Now you should go to see a real astronomer from the university and have him cast your horoscope so you know where you stand. (VIRGINIA *giggles.*) What's the matter?
VIRGINIA: I've been already.

87

MRS. SARTI: Tell Sarti.

VIRGINIA: I have to be careful for three months now because the sun is in Capricorn, but after that I get a favorable ascendant, and I can undertake a journey if I am careful of Uranus, as I'm a Scorpion.

MRS. SARTI: What about Ludovico?

VIRGINIA: He's a Leo, the astronomer said. Leos are sensual. (*Giggles.*)

There is a knock at the door, it opens. Enter the RECTOR OF THE UNIVERSITY, *the philosopher of Scene 4, bringing a book.*

RECTOR (*to* VIRGINIA): This is about the burning issue of the moment. He may want to glance over it. My faculty would appreciate his comments. No, don't disturb him now, my dear. Every minute one takes of your father's time is stolen from Italy. (*He goes.*)

VIRGINIA: Federzoni! The rector of the university brought this.

FEDERZONI *takes it.*

GALILEO: What's it about?

FEDERZONI (*spelling*): D-e m-a-c-u-l-i-s i-n s-o-l-e.

ANDREA: Oh, it's on the sun spots!

ANDREA *comes to one side, and the* LITTLE MONK *the other, to look at the book.*

ANDREA: A new one!

FEDERZONI *resentfully puts the book into their hands and continues with the preparation of the experiment.*

ANDREA: Listen to this dedication. (*Quotes:*) "To the greatest living authority on physics, Galileo Galilei." I read Fabricius' paper the other day. Fabricius says the spots are clusters of planets between us and the sun.

LITTLE MONK: Doubtful.

GALILEO (*noncommittal*): Yes?

ANDREA: Paris and Prague hold that they are vapors from the sun. Federzoni doubts that.

FEDERZONI: Me? You leave me out. I said "hm," that was all. And don't discuss new things before me. I can't read the material, it's in Latin. (*He drops the scales and stands trembling with fury.*) Tell me, can I doubt anything?

GALILEO *walks over and picks up the scales silently. Pause.*

LITTLE MONK: There is happiness in doubting, I wonder why.

ANDREA: Aren't we going to take this up?

GALILEO: At the moment we are investigating floating bodies.

ANDREA: Mother has baskets full of letters from all over Europe asking his opinion.

FEDERZONI: The question is whether you can afford to remain silent.

GALILEO: I cannot afford to be smoked on a wood fire like a ham.

ANDREA (*surprised*): Ah. You think the sun spots may have something to do with that again? (GALILEO *does not answer.*) Well, we stick to fiddling about with bits of ice in water. That can't hurt you.

GALILEO: Correct. Our thesis!

ANDREA: All things that are lighter than water float, and all things that are heavier sink.

GALILEO: Aristotle says—

LITTLE MONK (*reading out of a book, translating*): "A broad and flat disk of ice, although heavier than water, still floats, because it is unable to divide the water."

GALILEO: Well. Now I push the ice below the surface. I take away the pressure of my hands. What happens?

Pause.

LITTLE MONK: It rises to the surface.

GALILEO: Correct. It seems to be able to divide the water as it's coming up, doesn't it?

LITTLE MONK: Could it be lighter than water after all?

GALILEO: Aha!

ANDREA: Then all things that are lighter than water float, and all things that are heavier sink. Q.E.D.

GALILEO: Not at all. Hand me that iron needle. Heavier than water? (*They all nod.*) A piece of paper. (*He places the needle on a piece of paper and floats it on the surface of the water. Pause.*) Do not be hasty with your conclusion. (*Pause.*) What happens?

FEDERZONI: The paper has sunk, the needle is floating. (*They laugh.*)

VIRGINIA: What's the matter?

MRS. SARTI: Every time I hear them laugh it sends shivers down my spine.

There is a knocking at the outer door.

MRS. SARTI: Who's that at the door?

Enter LUDOVICO. VIRGINIA *runs to him. They embrace.* LUDOVICO *is followed by a* SERVANT *with baggage.*

MRS. SARTI: Well!

VIRGINIA: Oh! Why didn't you write that you were coming?

LUDOVICO: I decided on the spur of the moment. I was over inspecting our vineyards at Bucciole. I couldn't keep away.

GALILEO: Who's that?

LITTLE MONK: Miss Virginia's intended. What's the matter with your eyes?

GALILEO (*blinking*): Oh, yes, it's Ludovico, so it is. Well! Sarti, get a jug of that Sicilian wine, the old kind. We celebrate.

Everybody sits down. MRS. SARTI *has left, followed by* LUDOVICO'S SERVANT.

GALILEO: Well, Ludovico, old man. How are the horses?

LUDOVICO: The horses are fine.

GALILEO: Fine.

LUDOVICO: But those vineyards need a firm hand. (*To* VIRGINIA:) You look pale. Country life will suit you. Mother's planning on September.

VIRGINIA: I suppose I oughtn't, but stay here, I've got something to show you.

LUDOVICO: What?

VIRGINIA: Never mind. I won't be ten minutes. (*She runs out.*)

LUDOVICO: How's life these days, sir?

GALILEO: Dull. How was the journey?

LUDOVICO: Dull. Before I forget, mother sends her congratulations on your admirable tact over the latest rumblings of science.

GALILEO: Thank her from me.

LUDOVICO: Christopher Clavius had all Rome on its ears. He said he was afraid that the turning-around business might crop up again on account of these spots on the sun.

ANDREA: Clavius is on the same track! (*To* LUDOVICO:) My mother's baskets are full of letters from all over Europe asking Mr. Galilei's opinion.

GALILEO: I am engaged in investigating the habits of floating bodies. Any harm in that?

MRS. SARTI *re-enters, followed by the* SERVANT. *They bring wine and glasses on a tray.*

GALILEO (*hands out the wine*): What news from the Holy City, apart from the prospect of my sins?

LUDOVICO: The Holy Father is on his deathbed. Hadn't you heard?

LITTLE MONK: My goodness! What about the succession?

LUDOVICO: All the talk is of Barberini.

GALILEO: Barberini?

ANDREA: Mr. Galilei knows Barberini.

LITTLE MONK: Cardinal Barberini is a mathematician.

FEDERZONI: A scientist in the chair of Peter!

Pause.

GALILEO (*cheering up enormously*): This means change. We might live to see the day, Federzoni, when we don't have to whisper that two and two are four. (*To* LUDOVICO:) I like this wine. Don't you, Ludovico?

LUDOVICO: I like it.

GALILEO: I know the hill where it is grown. The slope is steep and stony, the grape almost blue. I am fond of this wine.

LUDOVICO. Yes, sir.

GALILEO: There are shadows in this wine. It is almost sweet but just stops short. . . . Andrea, clear that stuff away, ice, bowl, and needle. . . . I cherish the consolations of the flesh. I have no patience with cowards who call them weaknesses. I say there is a certain achievement in enjoying things.

The PUPILS *get up and go to the experiment table.*

LITTLE MONK: What are we to do?

FEDERZONI: He is starting on the sun.

They begin with clearing up.

ANDREA (*singing in a low voice*):

> The Bible proves the earth stands still,
> The Pope, he swears with tears:
> The earth stands still. To prove it so
> He takes it by the ears.

LUDOVICO: What's the excitement?

MRS. SARTI: You're not going to start those hellish goings-on again, Mr. Galilei?

ANDREA:

> And gentlefolk, they say so too.
> Each learned doctor proves
> (If you grease his palm): The earth stands still.
> And yet—and yet it moves.

GALILEO: Barberini is in the ascendant, so your mother is uneasy, and you're sent to investigate me. Correct me if I am wrong, Ludovico. Clavius is right: these spots on the sun interest me.

ANDREA: We might find out that the sun also revolves. How would you like that, Ludovico?

GALILEO: Do you like my wine, Ludovico?

LUDOVICO: I told you I did, sir.

GALILEO: You really like it?

LUDOVICO: I like it.

GALILEO: Tell me, Ludovico, would you consider going so far as to accept a man's wine or his daughter without insisting that he drop his profession? I have no wish to intrude, but have the moons of Jupiter affected Virginia's bottom?

MRS. SARTI: That isn't funny, it's just vulgar. I am going for Virginia.

LUDOVICO (keeps her back): Marriages in families such as mine are not arranged on a basis of sexual attraction alone.

GALILEO: Did they keep you back from marrying my daughter for eight years because I was on probation?

LUDOVICO: My future wife must take her place in the family pew.

GALILEO: You mean, if the daughter of a bad man sat in your family pew, your peasants might stop paying the rent?

LUDOVICO: In a sort of way.

GALILEO: When I was your age, the only person I allowed
to rap me on the knuckles was my girl.

LUDOVICO: My mother was assured that you had under-
taken not to get mixed up in this turning-around
business again, sir.

GALILEO: We had a conservative Pope then.

MRS. SARTI: Had! His Holiness is not dead yet!

GALILEO (*with relish*): Pretty nearly.

MRS. SARTI: That man will weigh a chip of ice fifty times,
but when it comes to something that's convenient, he
believes it blindly. "Is His Holiness dead?" "Pretty
nearly!"

LUDOVICO: You will find, sir, if His Holiness passes away,
the new Pope, whoever he turns out to be, will respect
the convictions held by the solid families of the
country.

GALILEO (*to* ANDREA): That remains to be seen. Andrea,
get out the screen. We'll throw the image of the sun
on our screen to save our eyes.

LITTLE MONK: I thought you'd been working at it. Do you
know when I guessed it? When you didn't recognize
Mr. Marsili.

MRS. SARTI: If my son has to go to hell for sticking to you,
that's my affair, but you have no right to trample on
your daughter's happiness.

LUDOVICO (*to his* SERVANT): Giuseppe, take my baggage
back to the coach, will you?

MRS. SARTI: This will kill her. (*She runs out, still clutching
the jug.*)

LUDOVICO (*politely*): Mr. Galilei, if we Marsilis were to
countenance teachings frowned on by the church, it
would unsettle our peasants. Bear in mind: these poor
people in their brute state get everything upside down.
They are nothing but animals. They will never com-
prehend the finer points of astronomy. Why, two
months ago a rumor went around an apple had been

found on a pear tree, and they left their work in the fields to discuss it.

GALILEO (*interested*): Did they?

LUDOVICO: I have seen the day when my poor mother has had to have a dog whipped before their eyes to remind them to keep their place. Oh, you may have seen the waving corn from the window of your comfortable coach. You have, no doubt, nibbled our olives, and absentmindedly eaten our cheese, but you can have no idea how much responsibility that sort of thing entails.

GALILEO: Young man, I do not eat my cheese absentmindedly. (*To* ANDREA:) Are we ready?

ANDREA: Yes, sir.

GALILEO (*leaves* LUDOVICO *and adjusts the mirror*): You would not confine your whippings to dogs to remind your peasants to keep their places, would you, Marsili?

LUDOVICO (*after a pause*): Mr. Galilei, you have a wonderful brain, it's a pity.

LITTLE MONK (*astonished*): He threatened you.

GALILEO: Yes. And he threatened you too. We might unsettle his peasants. Your sister, Fulganzio, who works the lever of the olive press, might laugh out loud if she heard the sun is not a gilded coat of arms but a lever too. The earth turns because the sun turns it.

ANDREA: That could interest his steward too and even his moneylender—and the seaport towns . . .

FEDERZONI: None of them speak Latin.

GALILEO: I might write in plain language. The work we do is exacting. Who would go through the strain for less than the population at large!

LUDOVICO: I see you have made your decision. It was inevitable. You will always be a slave of your passions. Excuse me to Virginia. I think it's as well I don't see her now.

GALILEO: The dowry is at your disposal at any time.

LUDOVICO: Good afternoon. (*He goes, followed by the* SERVANT.)

ANDREA: Exit Ludovico. To hell with all Marsilis, Villanis, Orsinis, Canes, Nuccolis, Soldanieris . . .

FEDERZONI: . . . who ordered the earth stand still because their castles might be shaken loose if it revolves . . .

LITTLE MONK: . . . and who only kiss the Pope's feet as long as he uses them to trample on the people. God made the physical world, God made the human brain. God will allow physics.

ANDREA: They will try to stop us.

GALILEO: Thus we enter the observation of these spots on the sun in which we are interested, at our own risk, not counting on protection from a problematical new Pope . . .

ANDREA: . . . but with great likelihood of dispelling Fabricius' vapors, and the shadows of Paris and Prague, and of establishing the rotation of the sun . . .

GALILEO: . . . and with *some* likelihood of establishing the rotation of the sun. My intention is not to prove that I was right but to find out *whether* I was right. "Abandon hope all ye who enter—an observation." Before assuming these phenomena are spots, which would suit us, let us first set about proving that they are not— fried fish. We crawl by inches. What we find today we will wipe from the blackboard tomorrow and reject it—unless it shows up again the day after tomorrow. And if we find anything which would suit us, that thing we will eye with particular distrust. In fact, we will approach this observing of the sun with the implacable determination to prove that the earth stands still, and only if hopelessly defeated in this pious undertaking can we allow ourselves to wonder if we may not have been right all the time: the earth revolves. Take the cloth off the telescope and turn it on the sun.

Quietly they start work. When the coruscating image of the sun is focused on the screen, VIRGINIA *enters hurriedly, her wedding dress on, her hair disheveled,* MRS. SARTI *with her, carrying her wedding veil. The two women realize what has happened.* VIRGINIA *faints.* ANDREA, LITTLE MONK, *and* GALILEO *rush to her.* FEDERZONI *continues working.*

SCENE 9

On April Fools' Day, thirty two,
Of science there was much ado.
People had learned from Galilei:
They used his teaching in their way.

Around the corner from the market place a BALLAD SINGER *and his* WIFE, *who is costumed to represent the earth in a skeleton globe made of thin bands of brass, are holding the attention of a sprinkling of representative citizens, some in masquerade, who were on their way to see the carnival procession. From the market place the noise of an impatient crowd.*

BALLAD SINGER (*accompanied by his* WIFE *on the guitar*):

When the Almighty made the universe
He made the earth and then he made the sun.
Then round the earth he bade the sun to turn—
That's in the Bible, Genesis, Chapter One.
And from that time all beings here below
Were in obedient circles meant to go:
    Around the pope the cardinals
    Around the cardinals the bishops
    Around the bishops the secretaries
    Around the secretaries the aldermen
    Around the aldermen the craftsmen
    Around the craftsmen the servants
    Around the servants the dogs, the chickens,
       and the beggars.

98

A conspicuous reveller—henceforth called the SPIN-
NER—has slowly caught on and is exhibiting his idea
of spinning around. He does not lose dignity, he faints
with mock grace.

BALLAD SINGER:

Up stood the learned Galileo
Glanced briefly at the sun
And said: "Almighty God was wrong
In Genesis, Chapter One!"
    Now that was rash, my friends, it is no matter small:
    For heresy will spread today like foul diseases.
    Change Holy Writ, forsooth? What will be left at all?
    Why: each of us would say and do just what he
        pleases!

Three wretched EXTRAS, *employed by the Chamber of*
Commerce, enter. Two of them, in ragged costumes,
moodily bear a litter with a mock throne. The third
sits on the throne. He wears sacking, a false beard, a
prop crown, he carries a prop orb and sceptre, and
around his chest the inscription "THE KING OF HUN-
GARY." *The litter has a card with "No. 4" written on*
it. The litter bearers dump him down and listen to
the BALLAD SINGER.

BALLAD SINGER:

Good people, what will come to pass
If Galileo's teachings spread?
No altar boy will serve the mass
No servant girl will make the bed.
    Now that is grave, my friends, it is no matter small:
    For independent spirit spreads like foul diseases!
    (Yet life is sweet and man is weak and after all—
    How nice it is, for a little change, to do just as one
        pleases!)

The BALLAD SINGER *takes over the guitar. His* WIFE
*dances around him, illustrating the motion of the earth.
A* COBBLER'S BOY *with a pair of resplendent lacquered
boots hung over his shoulder has been jumping up
and down in mock excitement. There are three more
children, dressed as grownups, among the spectators,
two together and a single one with mother. The* COB-
BLER'S BOY *takes the three* CHILDREN *in hand, forms a
chain and leads it, moving to the music, in and out
among the spectators, "whipping" the chain so that
the last child bumps into people. On the way past a*
PEASANT WOMAN, *he steals an egg from her basket.
She gestures to him to return it. As he passes her
again he quietly breaks the egg over her head. The*
KING OF HUNGARY *ceremoniously hands his orb to one
of his bearers, marches down with mock dignity, and
chastises the* COBBLER'S BOY. *The parents remove the
three* CHILDREN. *The unseemliness subsides.*

BALLAD SINGER:

The carpenters take wood and build
Their houses—not the church's pews.
And members of the cobblers' guild
Now boldly walk the streets—in shoes.
The tenant kicks the noble lord
Quite off the land he owned—like that!
The milk his wife once gave the priest
Now makes (at last!) her children fat.
   Ts, ts, ts, ts, my friends, this is no matter small:
   For independent spirit spreads like foul diseases.
   People must keep their place, some down and some
     on top!
   (Though it is nice, for a little change, to do just as
     one pleases!)

The COBBLER'S BOY *has put on the lacquered boots he*

was carrying. He struts off. The BALLAD SINGER *takes
over the guitar again. His* WIFE *dances around him in
increased tempo. A* MONK *has been standing near a*
RICH COUPLE, *who are in subdued, costly clothes,
without masks; shocked at the song, he now leaves. A*
DWARF *in the costume of an astronomer turns his telescope on the departing* MONK, *thus drawing attention
to the* RICH COUPLE. *In imitation of the* COBBLER'S
BOY, *the* SPINNER *forms a chain of grownups. They
move to the music, in and out, and between the* RICH
COUPLE. *The* SPINNER *changes the gentleman's bonnet
for the ragged hat of a beggar. The* GENTLEMAN *de-
cides to take this in good part, and a* GIRL *is embold-
ened to take his dagger. The* GENTLEMAN *is miffed,
throws the beggar's hat back. The* BEGGAR *discards the
gentleman's bonnet and drops it on the ground. The*
KING OF HUNGARY *has walked from his throne, taken
an egg from the* PEASANT WOMAN, *and paid for it. He
now ceremoniously breaks it over the gentleman's
head as he is bending down to pick up his bonnet.
The* GENTLEMAN *conducts the* LADY *away from the
scene. The* KING OF HUNGARY, *about to resume his
throne, finds one of the* CHILDREN *sitting on it. The*
GENTLEMAN *returns to retrieve his dagger. Merriment.
The* BALLAD SINGER *wanders off. This is part of his
routine. His* WIFE *sings to the* SPINNER.

WIFE:

Now speaking for myself I feel
That I could also do with a change.
You know, for me—(*turning to a reveller*)—you have
   appeal
Maybe tonight we could arrange . . .

The DWARF-ASTRONOMER *has been amusing the peo-*

ple by focusing his telescope on her legs. The BALLAD
SINGER *has returned.*

BALLAD SINGER:

No, no, no, no, no, stop, Galileo, stop!
For independent spirit spreads like foul diseases.
People must keep their place, some down and some on
top!
(Though it is nice, for a little change, to do just as one
pleases!)

The SPECTATORS *stand embarrassed. A* GIRL *laughs
loudly.*

BALLAD SINGER AND HIS WIFE:

Good people who have trouble here below
In serving cruel lords and gentle Jesus
Who bids you turn the other cheek just so . . . (*With
mimicry.*)
While they prepare to strike the second blow:
Obedience will never cure your woe
So each of you wake up and do just as he pleases!

The BALLAD SINGER *and his* WIFE *hurriedly start to
try to sell pamphlets to the spectators.*

BALLAD SINGER: Read all about the earth going round the
sun, two centesimi only. As proved by the great
Galileo. Two centesimi only. Written by a local
scholar. Understandable to one and all. Buy one for
your friends, your children and your Aunty Rosa,
two centesimi only. Abbreviated but complete. Fully
illustrated with pictures of the planets, including
Venus, two centesimi only.

During the speech of the BALLAD SINGER *we hear the carnival procession approaching, followed by laughter. A* REVELLER *rushes in.*

REVELLER: The procession!

The litter bearers speedily joggle out the KING OF HUNGARY. *The* SPECTATORS *turn and look at the first float of the procession, which now makes its appearance. It bears a gigantic figure of* GALILEO, *holding in one hand an open Bible with the pages crossed out. The other hand points to the Bible, and the head mechanically turns from side to side as if to say "No! No!"*

A LOUD VOICE: Galileo, the Bible-killer!

The laughter from the market place becomes uproarious. The MONK *comes flying from the market place followed by delighted* CHILDREN.

SCENE 10

The depths are hot, the heights are chill,
The streets are loud, the court is still.

Antechamber and staircase in the Medicean palace in Florence. GALILEO, *with a book under his arm, waits with his daughter* VIRGINIA *to be admitted to the presence of the* PRINCE.

VIRGINIA: They are a long time.

GALILEO: Yes.

VIRGINIA: Who is that funny-looking man? (*She indicates the* INFORMER, *who has entered casually, and seated himself in the background, taking no apparent notice of* GALILEO.)

GALILEO: I don't know.

VIRGINIA: It's not the first time I have seen him around. He gives me the creeps.

GALILEO: Nonsense. We're in Florence, not among robbers in the mountains of Corsica.

VIRGINIA: Here comes the Rector.

The RECTOR *comes down the stairs.*

GALILEO: Gaffone is a bore. He attaches himself to you.

The RECTOR *passes, scarcely nodding.*

GALILEO: My eyes are bad today. Did he acknowledge us?

VIRGINIA: Barely. (*Pause.*) What's in your book? Will they say it's heretical?

GALILEO: You hang around church too much. And getting
up at dawn and scurrying to mass is ruining your
skin. You pray for me, don't you?

A MAN *comes down the stairs.*

VIRGINIA: Here's Mr. Matti. You designed a machine for
his iron foundries.

MATTI: How were the squabs, Mr. Galilei? (*Low*:) My
brother and I had a good laugh the other day. He
picked up a racy pamphlet against the Bible somewhere. It quoted you.

GALILEO: The squabs, Matti, were wonderful, thank you
again. Pamphlets I know nothing about. The Bible
and Homer are my favorite reading.

MATTI: No necessity to be cautious with me, Mr. Galilei.
I am on your side. I am not a man who knows about
the motions of the stars, but you have championed the
freedom to teach new things. Take that mechanical
cultivator they have in Germany which you described
to me. I can tell you, it will never be used in this
country. The same circles that are hampering you
now will forbid the physicians at Bologna to cut up
corpses for research. Do you know, they have such
things as money markets in Amsterdam and in London? Schools for business, too. Regular papers with
news. Here we are not even free to make money. I
have a stake in your career. They are against iron
foundries because they say the gathering of so many
workers in one place fosters immorality! If they
ever try anything, Mr. Galilei, remember you have
friends in all walks of life, including an iron founder.
Good luck to you. (*He goes.*)

GALILEO: Good man, but need he be so affectionate in
public? His voice carries. They will always claim me
as their spiritual leader, particularly in places where
it doesn't help me at all. I have written a book about

the mechanics of the firmament, that is all. What they
do or don't do with it is not my concern.

VIRGINIA (*loud*): If people only knew how you disagreed
with those goings-on all over the country last All
Fools' day.

GALILEO: Yes. Offer honey to a bear, and lose your arm
if the beast is hungry.

VIRGINIA (*low*): Did the Prince ask you to come here
today?

GALILEO: I sent word I was coming. He will want the
book, he has paid for it. My health hasn't been any
too good lately. I may accept Sagredo's invitation to
stay with him in Padua for a few weeks.

VIRGINIA: You couldn't manage without your books.

GALILEO: Sagredo has an excellent library.

VIRGINIA: We haven't had this month's salary yet—

GALILEO: Yes. (*The* CARDINAL INQUISITOR *passes down
the staircase. He bows deeply in answer to Galileo's
bow.*) What is he doing in Florence? If they try to do
anything to me, the new Pope will meet them with an
iron NO. And the Prince is my pupil, he would never
have me extradited.

VIRGINIA: Psst. The Lord Chamberlain.

The LORD CHAMBERLAIN *comes down the stairs.*

LORD CHAMBERLAIN: His Highness had hoped to find time
for you, Mr. Galilei. Unfortunately, he has to leave
immediately to judge the parade at the Riding Acad-
emy. On what business did you wish to see His Highness?

GALILEO: I wanted to present my book to His Highness.

LORD CHAMBERLAIN: How are your eyes today?

GALILEO: So, so. With His Highness' permission, I am
dedicating the book . . .

LORD CHAMBERLAIN: Your eyes are a matter of great concern to His Highness. Could it be that you have been

looking too long and too often through your marvelous tube? (*He leaves without accepting the book.*)

VIRGINIA (*greatly agitated*): Father, I am afraid.

GALILEO: He didn't take the book, did he? (*Low and resolute*:) Keep a straight face. We are not going home, but to the house of the lens-grinder. There is a coach and horses in his backyard. Keep your eyes to the front, don't look back at that man.

They start. The LORD CHAMBERLAIN *comes back.*

LORD CHAMBERLAIN: Oh, Mr. Galilei, His Highness has just charged me to inform you that the Florentine court is no longer in a position to oppose the request of the Holy Inquisition to interrogate you in Rome.

SCENE 11

The Pope

A chamber in the Vatican. The POPE, URBAN VIII—
formerly Cardinal Barberini—is giving audience to the
CARDINAL INQUISITOR. *The trampling and shuffling of many
feet is heard throughout the scene from the adjoining cor-
ridors. During the scene the* POPE *is being robed for the
conclave he is about to attend: at the beginning of the scene
he is plainly Barberini, but as the scene proceeds he is
more and more obscured by grandiose vestments.*

POPE: No! No! No!

INQUISITOR (*referring to the owners of the shuffling feet*):
Doctors of all chairs from the universities, representa-
tives of the special orders of the Church, represen-
tatives of the clergy as a whole, who have come
believing with childlike faith in the word of God as
set forth in the Scriptures, who have come to hear
Your Holiness confirm their faith: and Your Holiness
is really going to tell them that the Bible can no
longer be regarded as the alphabet of truth?

POPE: I will not set myself up against the multiplication
table. No!

INQUISITOR: Ah, that is what these people say, that it is
the multiplication table. Their cry is, "The figures
compel us," but where do these figures come from?
Plainly they come from doubt. These men doubt
everything. Can society stand on doubt and not on
faith? "Thou are my master, but I doubt whether

it is for the best." "This is my neighbor's house and my neighbor's wife, but why shouldn't they belong to me?" After the plague, after the new war, after the unparalleled disaster of the Reformation, your dwindling flock look to their shepherd, and now the mathematicians turn their tubes on the sky and announce to the world that you have not the best advice about the heavens either—up to now your only uncontested sphere of influence. This Galilei started meddling in machines at an early age. Now that men in ships are venturing on the great oceans—I am not against that of course—they are putting their faith in a brass bowl they call a compass and not in Almighty God.

POPE: This man is the greatest physicist of our time. He is the light of Italy, and not just any muddlehead.

INQUISITOR: Would we have had to arrest him otherwise? This bad man knows what he doing, not writing his books in Latin, but in the jargon of the market place.

POPE (*occupied with the shuffling feet*): That was not in the best of taste. (*A pause.*) These shuffling feet are making me nervous.

INQUISITOR: May they be more telling than my words, Your Holiness. Shall all these go from you with doubt in their hearts?

POPE: This man has friends. What about Versailles?* What about the Viennese court? They will call Holy Church a cesspool for defunct ideas. Keep your hands off him.

INQUISITOR: In practice it will never get far. He is a man of the flesh. He would soften at once.

POPE: He has more enjoyment in him than any man I ever saw. He loves eating and drinking and thinking. To excess. He indulges in thinking-bouts! He cannot say no to an old wine or a new thought. (*Furious:*) I

---

*An anachronism but Brecht's own. —E. B.

do not want a condemnation of physical facts. I do not want to hear battle cries: Church, Church, Church! Reason, Reason, Reason! (*Pause.*) These shuffling feet are intolerable. Has the whole world come to my door?

INQUISITOR: Not the whole world, Your Holiness. A select gathering of the faithful.

Pause.

POPE (*exhausted*): It is clearly understood: he is not to be tortured. (*Pause.*) At the very most, he may be shown the instruments.

INQUISITOR: That will be adequate, Your Holiness. Mr. Galilei understands machinery.

The eyes of BARBERINI *look helplessly at the* CARDINAL INQUISITOR *from under the completely assembled panoply of* POPE URBAN VIII.

SCENE 12

June twenty second, sixteen thirty three,
A momentous date for you and me.
Of all the days that was the one
An age of reason could have begun.

Again the garden of the Florentine AMBASSADOR *at Rome, where Galileo's assistants wait the news of the trial. The* LITTLE MONK *and* FEDERZONI *are attempting to concentrate on a game of chess.* VIRGINIA *kneels in a corner, praying and counting her beads.*

LITTLE MONK: The Pope didn't even grant him an audience.

FEDERZONI: No more scientific discussions.

ANDREA: The "Discorsi" will never be finished. The sum of his findings. They will kill him.

FEDERZONI (*stealing a glance at him*): Do you really think so?

ANDREA: He will never recant.

Silence.

LITTLE MONK: You know when you lie awake at night how your mind fastens on to something irrelevant. Last night I kept thinking: if only they would let him take his little stone in with him, the appeal-to-reason-pebble that he always carries in his pocket.

FEDERZONI: In the room *they'll* take him to, he won't have a pocket.

ANDREA: But he will not recant.

LITTLE MONK: How can they beat the truth out of a man

who gave his sight in order to see?
FEDERZONI: Maybe they can't.

Silence.

ANDREA (*speaking about* VIRGINIA): She is praying that he will recant.
FEDERZONI: Leave her alone. She doesn't know whether she's on her head or on her heels since they got hold of her. They brought her Father Confessor from Florence.

The INFORMER *of Scene 10 enters.*

INFORMER: Mr. Galilei will be here soon. He may need a bed.
FEDERZONI: Have they let him out?
INFORMER: Mr. Galilei is expected to recant at five o'clock. The big bell of Saint Marcus will be rung and the complete text of his recantation publicly announced.
ANDREA: I don't believe it.
INFORMER: Mr. Galilei will be brought to the garden gate at the back of the house, to avoid the crowds collecting in the streets. (*He goes.*)

Silence.

ANDREA: The moon is an earth because the light of the moon is not her own. Jupiter is a fixed star, and four moons turn around Jupiter, therefore we are not shut in by crystal shells. The sun is the pivot of our world, therefore the earth is not the center. The earth moves, spinning about the sun. And he showed us. You can't make a man unsee what he has seen.

Silence.

FEDERZONI: Five o'clock is one minute.

VIRGINIA *prays louder.*

ANDREA: Listen all of you, they are murdering the truth.

He stops up his ears with his fingers. The two other pupils do the same. FEDERZONI *goes over to the* LITTLE MONK, *and all of them stand absolutely still in cramped positions. Nothing happens. No bell sounds. After a silence, filled with the murmur of Virginia's prayers,* FEDERZONI *runs to the wall to look at the clock. He turns around, his expression changed. He shakes his head. They drop their hands.*

FEDERZONI: No. No bell. It is three minutes after.
LITTLE MONK: He hasn't.
ANDREA: He held true. It is all right, it is all right.
LITTLE MONK: He did not recant.
FEDERZONI: No.

They embrace each other, they are delirious with joy.

ANDREA: So force cannot accomplish everything. What has been seen can't be unseen. Man is constant in the face of death.
FEDERZONI: June 22, 1633: dawn of the age of reason. I wouldn't have wanted to go on living if he had recanted.
LITTLE MONK: I didn't say anything, but I was in agony. O ye of little faith!
ANDREA: I was sure.
FEDERZONI: It would have turned our morning to night.
ANDREA: It would have been as if the mountain had turned to water.
LITTLE MONK (*kneeling down, crying*): O God, I thank Thee.
ANDREA: Beaten humanity can lift its head. A man has stood up and said No.

At this moment the bell of Saint Marcus begins to toll. They stand like statues VIRGINIA *stands up.*

114 / Galileo

VIRGINIA: The bell of Saint Marcus. He is not damned.

From the street one hears the TOWN CRIER *reading* GALILEO'S *recantation.*

TOWN CRIER: I, Galileo Galilei, Teacher of Mathematics and Physics, do hereby publicly renounce my teaching that the earth moves. I forswear this teaching with a sincere heart and unfeigned faith and detest and curse this and all other errors and heresies repugnant to the Holy Scriptures.

The lights dim; when they come up again the bell of Saint Marcus is petering out. VIRGINIA *has gone but the* SCHOLARS *are still there waiting.*

ANDREA (*loud*): The mountain did turn to water.

GALILEO *has entered quietly and unnoticed. He is changed, almost unrecognizable. He has heard* ANDREA. *He waits some seconds by the door for somebody to greet him. Nobody does. They retreat from him. He goes slowly and, because of his bad sight, uncertainly, to the front of the stage, where he finds a chair and sits down.*

ANDREA: I can't look at him. Tell him to go away.
FEDERZONI: Steady.
ANDREA (*hysterically*): He saved his big gut.
FEDERZONI: Get him a glass of water.

The LITTLE MONK *fetches a glass of water for* ANDREA. *Nobody acknowledges the presence of* GALILEO, *who sits silently on his chair listening to the voice of the* TOWN CRIER, *now in another street.*

ANDREA: I can walk. Just help me a bit.

They help him to the door.

ANDREA (*in the door*): "Unhappy is the land that breeds no hero."

GALILEO: No, Andrea: "Unhappy is the land that needs a hero."

Before the next scene, a curtain with the following legend on it is lowered:

> YOU CAN PLAINLY SEE THAT IF A HORSE WERE TO
> FALL FROM A HEIGHT OF THREE OR FOUR FEET, IT
> COULD BREAK ITS BONES, WHEREAS A DOG WOULD
> NOT SUFFER INJURY. THE SAME APPLIES TO A CAT
> FROM A HEIGHT OF AS MUCH AS EIGHT OR TEN
> FEET, TO A GRASSHOPPER FROM THE TOP OF A
> TOWER, AND TO AN ANT FALLING DOWN FROM
> THE MOON. NATURE COULD NOT ALLOW A HORSE
> TO BECOME AS BIG AS TWENTY HORSES NOR A
> GIANT AS BIG AS TEN MEN, UNLESS SHE WERE TO
> CHANGE THE PROPORTIONS OF ALL ITS MEMBERS,
> PARTICULARLY THE BONES. THUS THE COMMON
> ASSUMPTION THAT GREAT AND SMALL STRUCTURES
> ARE EQUALLY TOUGH IS OBVIOUSLY WRONG.
>
> —FROM THE "DISCORSI"

SCENE 13

1633-1642
*Galileo Galilei remains a prisoner
of the Inquisition until his death.*

*A country house near Florence. A large room simply
furnished. There is a huge table, a leather chair, a globe
of the world on a stand, and a narrow bed. A portion of
the adjoining anteroom is visible, and the front door, which
opens into it. An* OFFICIAL *of the Inquisition sits on guard
in the anteroom. In the large room,* GALILEO *is quietly
experimenting with a bent wooden rail and a small ball
of wood. He is still vigorous but almost blind. After a while
there is a knocking at the outside door. The* OFFICIAL
opens it to a PEASANT *who brings a plucked goose.* VIRGINIA
comes from the kitchen. She is past forty.

PEASANT (*handing the goose to* VIRGINIA): I was told to
   deliver this here.
VIRGINIA: I didn't order a goose.
PEASANT: I was told to say it's from someone who was
   passing through.

> VIRGINIA *takes the goose, surprised. The* OFFICIAL
> *takes it from her and examines it suspiciously. Then,
> reassured, he hands it back to her. The* PEASANT *goes.*
> VIRGINIA *brings the goose in to* GALILEO.

VIRGINIA: Somebody who was passing through sent you
   something.
GALILEO: What is it?

VIRGINIA: Can't you see it?

GALILEO: No. (*He walks over.*) A goose. Any name?

VIRGINIA: No.

GALILEO (*weighing the goose*): Solid.

VIRGINIA (*cautiously*): Will you eat the liver, if I have it cooked with a little apple?

GALILEO: I had my dinner. Are you under orders to finish me off with food?

VIRGINIA: It's not rich. And what is wrong with your eyes again? You should be able to see it.

GALILEO: You were standing in the light.

VIRGINIA: I was not. You haven't been writing again?

GALILEO (*sneering*): What do you think?

VIRGINIA *takes the goose out into the anteroom and speaks to the* OFFICIAL.

VIRGINIA: You had better ask Monsignor Carpula to send the doctor. Father couldn't see this goose across the room. Don't look at me like that. He has not been writing. He dictates everything to me, as you know.

OFFICIAL: Yes?

VIRGINIA: He abides by the rules. My father's repentance is sincere. I keep an eye on him. (*She hands him the goose.*) Tell the cook to fry the liver with an apple and an onion. (*She goes back into the large room.*) And you have no business to be doing that with those eyes of yours, father.

GALILEO: You may read me some Horace.

VIRGINIA: We should go on with your weekly letter to the Archbishop. Monsignor Carpula, to whom we owe so much, was all smiles the other day because the Archbishop had expressed his pleasure at your collaboration.

GALILEO: Where were we?

VIRGINIA (*sits down to take his dictation*): Paragraph four.

GALILEO: Read what you have.

VIRGINIA: "The position of the Church in the matter of the unrest at Genoa. I agree with Cardinal Spoletti in the matter of the unrest among the Venetian rope-makers . . ."

GALILEO: Yes. (*Dictates:*) I agree with Cardinal Spoletti in the matter of the unrest among the Venetian rope-makers: it is better to distribute good, nourishing food in the name of charity than to pay them more for their bell ropes. It being surely better to strengthen their faith than to encourage their acquisitiveness. St. Paul says: Charity never faileth. . . . How is that?

VIRGINIA: It's beautiful, father.

GALILEO: It couldn't be taken as irony?

VIRGINIA: No. The Archbishop will like it. It's so practical.

GALILEO: I trust your judgment. Read it over slowly.

VIRGINIA: "The position of the Church in the matter of the unrest—"

There is a knocking at the outside door. VIRGINIA *goes into the anteroom. The* OFFICIAL *opens the door. It is* ANDREA.

ANDREA: Good evening. I am sorry to call so late, I'm on my way to Holland. I was asked to look him up. Can I go in?

VIRGINIA: I don't know whether he will see you. You never came.

ANDREA: Ask him.

GALILEO *recognizes the voice. He sits motionless.* VIRGINIA *comes in to* GALILEO.

GALILEO: Is that Andrea?

VIRGINIA: Yes. (*Pause.*) I will send him away.

GALILEO: Show him in.

VIRGINIA *shows* ANDREA *in.* VIRGINIA *sits,* ANDREA *remains standing.*

ANDREA (*cool*): Have you been keeping well, Mr. Galilei?

GALILEO: Sit down. What are you doing these days? What are you working on? I heard it was something about hydraulics in Milan.

ANDREA: As he knew I was passing through, Fabricius of Amsterdam asked me to visit you and inquire about your health.

Pause.

GALILEO: I am very well.

ANDREA (*formally*): I am glad I can report you are in good health.

GALILEO: Fabricius will be glad to hear it. And you might inform him that, on account of the depth of my repentance, I live in comparative comfort.

ANDREA· Yes, we understand that the Church is more than pleased with you. Your complete acceptance has had its effect. Not one paper expounding a new thesis has made its appearance in Italy since your submission.

Pause.

GALILEO: Unfortunately there are countries not under the wing of the Church. Would you not say the erroneous, condemned theories are still taught—there?

ANDREA (*relentless*): Things are almost at a standstill.

GALILEO: Are they? (*Pause.*) Nothing from Descartes in Paris?

ANDREA: Yes. On receiving the news of your recantation, he shelved his treatise on the nature of light.

GALILEO: I sometimes worry about my assistants, whom I led into error. Have they benefited by my example?

ANDREA: In order to work I have to go to Holland.

GALILEO: Yes.

ANDREA: Federzoni is grinding lenses again, back in some shop.

GALILEO: He can't read the books.

ANDREA: Fulganzio, our little monk, has abandoned research and is resting in peace in the Church.

GALILEO: So. (*Pause.*) My superiors are looking forward to my spiritual recovery. I am progressing as well as can be expected.

VIRGINIA: You are doing well, father.

GALILEO: Virginia, leave the room.

VIRGINIA *rises uncertainly and goes out.*

VIRGINIA (*to the* OFFICIAL): He was his pupil, so now he is his enemy. Help me in the kitchen.

She leaves the anteroom with the OFFICIAL.

ANDREA: May I go now, sir?

GALILEO: I do not know why you came, Sarti. To unsettle me? I have to be prudent.

ANDREA: I'll be on my way.

GALILEO: As it is, I have relapses. I completed the "Discorsi."

ANDREA: You completed what?

GALILEO: My "Discorsi."

ANDREA: How?

GALILEO: I am allowed pen and paper. My superiors are intelligent men. They know the habits of a lifetime cannot be broken abruptly. But they protect me from any unpleasant consequences: they lock my pages away as I dictate them. And I should know better than to risk my comfort. I wrote the "Discorsi" out again during the night. The manuscript is in the globe. My vanity has up to now prevented me from destroying it. If you consider taking it, you will shoulder the entire risk. You will say it was pirated from the original in the hands of the Holy Office.

ANDREA, *as in a trance, has gone to the globe. He lifts the upper half and gets the book. He turns the pages as if wanting to devour them. In the back-ground the opening sentences of the "Discorsi" appear:*

MY PURPOSE IS TO SET FORTH A VERY NEW SCIENCE DEALING WITH A VERY ANCIENT SUBJECT—MOTION. . . . AND I HAVE DISCOVERED BY EXPERIMENT SOME PROPERTIES OF IT WHICH ARE WORTH KNOWING. . . .

GALILEO: I had to employ my time somehow.

The text disappears.

ANDREA: Two new sciences! This will be the foundation stone of a new physics.

GALILEO: Yes. Put it under your coat.

ANDREA: And we thought you had deserted. (*In a low voice:*) Mr. Galilei, how can I begin to express my shame. Mine has been the loudest voice against you.

GALILEO: That would seem to have been proper. I taught you science and I decried the truth.

ANDREA: Did you? I think not. Everything is changed!

GALILEO: What is changed?

ANDREA: You shielded the truth from the oppressor. Now I see! In your dealings with the Inquisition you used the same superb common sense you brought to physics.

GALILEO: Oh!

ANDREA: We lost our heads. With the crowd at the street corners we said: "He will die, he will never surrender!" You came back: "I surrendered but I am alive." We cried: "Your hands are stained!" You say: "Better stained than empty."

GALILEO: "Better stained than empty." It sounds realistic. Sounds like me.

ANDREA: And I of all people should have known. I was twelve when you sold another man's telescope to the

Venetian Senate, and saw you put it to immortal use. Your friends were baffled when you bowed to the Prince of Florence: science gained a wider audience. You always laughed at heroics. "People who suffer bore me," you said. "Misfortunes are due mainly to miscalculations." And: "If there are obstacles, the shortest line between two points may be the crooked line."

GALILEO: It makes a picture.

ANDREA: And when you stooped to recant in 1633, I should have understood that you were again about your business.

GALILEO: My business being?

ANDREA: Science. The study of the properties of motion, mother of the machines which will themselves change the ugly face of the earth.

GALILEO: Aha!

ANDREA: You gained time to write a book that only you could write. Had you burned at the stake in a blaze of glory they would have won.

GALILEO: They have won. And there is no such thing as a scientific work that only one man can write.

ANDREA: Then why did you recant, tell me that!

GALILEO: I recanted because I was afraid of physical pain.

ANDREA: No!

GALILEO: They showed me the instruments.

ANDREA: It was not a plan?

GALILEO: It was not.

Pause.

ANDREA: But you have contributed. Science has only one commandment: contribution. And you have contributed more than any man for a hundred years.

GALILEO: Have I? Then welcome to my gutter, dear colleague in science and brother in treason: I sold out, you are a buyer. The first sight of the book! His mouth watered and his scoldings were drowned. Blessed be our bargaining, whitewashing, death-fearing community!

ANDREA: The fear of death is human.

GALILEO: Even the Church will teach you that to be weak is not human. It is just evil.

ANDREA: The Church, yes! But science is not concerned with our weaknesses.

GALILEO: No? My dear Sarti, in spite of my present convictions, I may be able to give you a few pointers as to the concerns of your chosen profession. (*Enter* VIRGINIA *with a platter*.) In my spare time, I happen to have gone over this case. I have spare time. Even a man who sells wool, however good he is at buying wool cheap and selling it dear, must be concerned with the standing of the wool trade. The practice of science would seem to call for valor. She trades in knowledge, which is the product of doubt. And this new art of doubt has enchanted the public. The plight of the multitude is old as the rocks, and is believed to be basic as the rocks. But now they have learned to doubt. They snatched the telescopes out of our hands and had them trained on their tormentors: prince, official, public moralist. The mechanism of the heavens was clearer, the mechanism of their courts was still murky. The battle to measure the heavens is won by doubt; by credulity the Roman housewife's battle for milk will always be lost. Word is passed down that this is of no concern to the scientist, who is told he will only release such of his findings as do not disturb the peace, that is, the peace of mind of the well-to-do. Threats and bribes fill the air. Can the scientist hold out on the numbers? For what reason do you labor? I take it that the intent of science is to ease human existence. If you give way to coercion, science can be crippled, and your new machines may simply suggest new drudgeries. Should you, then, in time, discover all there is to be discovered, your progress must become a progress away from the bulk of humanity. The gulf might even grow so wide that the sound of your cheering at some new achievement would be echoed by a universal howl of horror. As a scientist I had an almost unique opportunity. In my day astronomy emerged into the market place. At that particular time, had one man put up a fight, it could have had wide repercussions. I have come to believe that I was never in real danger; for some years I was as strong as the authorities, and I surrendered my knowledge to the powers that be, to use it, no, not *use* it, *abuse* it, as it suits their ends. I have betrayed my profession. Any man who does what I have done must not be tolerated in the ranks of science.

VIRGINIA, *who has stood motionless, puts the platter on the table.*

VIRGINIA: You are accepted in the ranks of the faithful, father.

GALILEO (*sees her*): Correct. (*He goes over to the table.*) I have to eat now.

VIRGINIA: We lock up at eight.

ANDREA: I am glad I came. (*He extends his hand.* GALILEO *ignores it and goes over to his meal.*)

GALILEO (*examining the plate; to* ANDREA): Somebody who knows me sent me a goose. I still enjoy eating.

ANDREA: And your opinion is now that the "new age" was an illusion?

GALILEO: Well. This age of ours turned out to be a whore, spattered with blood. Maybe, new ages look like blood-spattered whores. Take care of yourself.

ANDREA: Yes. (*Unable to go.*) With reference to your evaluation of the author in question—I do not know

the answer. But I cannot think that your savage
analysis is the last word.

GALILEO: Thank you, sir.

OFFICIAL *knocks at the door.*

VIRGINIA (*showing* ANDREA *out*): I don't like visitors from
the past, they excite him.

She lets him out. The OFFICIAL *closes the iron door.*
VIRGINIA *returns.*

GALILEO (*eating*): Did you try and think who sent the
goose?

VIRGINIA: Not Andrea.

GALILEO: Maybe not. I gave Redhead his first lesson; when
he held out his hand, I had to remind myself he is
teaching now. How is the sky tonight?

VIRGINIA (*at the window*): Bright.

GALILEO *continues eating.*

SCENE 14

The great book o'er the border went
And, good folk, that was the end.
But we hope you'll keep in mind
You and I were left behind.

Before a little Italian customs house early in the morning.
ANDREA *sits upon one of his traveling trunks at the barrier
and read Galileo's book. The window of a small house is
still lit, and a big grotesque shadow, like an old witch and
her cauldron, falls upon the house wall beyond. Barefoot*
CHILDREN *in rags see it and point to the little house.*

CHILDREN (*singing*):

> One, two, three, four, five, six,
> Old Marina is a witch.
> At night, on a broomstick she sits
> And on the church steeple she spits.

CUSTOMS OFFICER (*to* ANDREA): Why are you making this
journey?

ANDREA: I am a scholar.

CUSTOMS OFFICER (*to his* CLERK): Put down under
"Reason for Leaving the Country": Scholar. (*He
points to the baggage*:) Books! Anything dangerous
in these books?

ANDREA: What is dangerous?

CUSTOMS OFFICER: Religion. Politics.

ANDREA: These are nothing but mathematical formulas.

CUSTOMS OFFICER: What's that?

ANDREA: Figures.

CUSTOMS OFFICER: Oh, figures. No harm in figures. Just
wait a minute, sir, we will soon have your papers
stamped. (*He exits with* CLERK.)

Meanwhile, a little council of war among the CHILDREN
has taken place. ANDREA *quietly watches. One of the*
BOYS, *pushes forward by the others, creeps up to the*
little house from which the shadow comes, and takes
the jug of milk on the doorstep.

ANDREA (*quietly*): What are you doing with that milk?

BOY (*stopping in mid-movement*): She is a witch.

The other CHILDREN *run away behind the customs*
house. One of them shouts, "Run, Paolo!"

ANDREA: Hmm! And because she is a witch she mustn't
have milk. Is that the idea?

BOY: Yes.

ANDREA: And how do you know she is a witch?

BOY (*points to shadow on house wall*): Look!

ANDREA: Oh! I see.

BOY: And she rides on a broomstick at night—and she
bewitches the coachman's horses. My cousin Luigi
looked through the hole in the stable roof, that the
snow storm made, and heard the horses coughing
something terrible.

ANDREA: Oh! How big was the hole in the stable roof?

BOY: Luigi didn't tell. Why?

ANDREA: I was asking because maybe the horses got sick
because it was cold in the stable. You had better ask
Luigi how big that hole is.

BOY: You are not going to say Old Marina isn't a witch,
because you can't.

ANDREA: No, I can't say she isn't a witch. I haven't looked
into it. A man can't know about a thing he hasn't
looked into, or can he?

BOY: No! But THAT! (*He points to the shadow.*) She is stirring hellbroth.

ANDREA: Let's see. Do you want to take a look? I can lift you up.

BOY: You lift me to the window, mister! (*He takes a sling-shot out of his pocket.*) I can really bash her from there.

ANDREA: Hadn't we better make sure she is a witch before we shoot? I'll hold that.

The BOY puts the milk jug down and follows him reluctantly to the window. ANDREA lifts the boy up so that he can look in.

ANDREA: What do you see?

BOY (*slowly*): Just an old girl cooking porridge.

ANDREA: Oh! Nothing to it then. Now look at her shadow, Paolo.

The BOY looks over his shoulder and back and compares the reality and the shadow.

BOY: The big thing is a soup ladle.

ANDREA: Ah! A ladle! You see, I would have taken it for a broomstick, but I haven't looked into the matter as you have, Paolo. Here is your sling.

CUSTOMS OFFICER (*returning with the CLERK and handing ANDREA his papers*): All present and correct. Good luck, sir.

ANDREA goes, reading Galileo's book. The CLERK starts to bring his baggage after him. The barrier rises. ANDREA passes through, still reading the book. The BOY kicks over the milk jug.

BOY (*shouting after ANDREA*): She *is* a witch! She *is* a witch!

ANDREA: You saw with your own eyes: think it over!

The BOY *joins the others. They sing.*

> One, two, three, four, five, six,
> Old Marina is a witch.
> At night, on a broomstick she sits
> And on the church steeple she spits.

The CUSTOMS OFFICERS *laugh.* ANDREA *goes.*

> *May you now guard science' light,*
> *Kindle it and use it right,*
> *Lest it be a flame to fall*
> *Downward to consume us all.*

APPENDIX A

Appendix A

WRITING THE TRUTH: FIVE DIFFICULTIES

Bertolt Brecht

[*The first version of this essay was a contribution to a questionnaire in the* Pariser Tageblatt, *December 12, 1934, which bore the general title "Dichter sollen die Wahrheit schreiben" ("Poets Are to Tell the Truth"). In it, Brecht proposed only three difficulties. The final version of the essay, here translated, had its first German publication in* Unsere Zeit (Paris), *VIII, Nos. 2/3 (April, 1935), 23-34. The translation first appeared in* Twice A Year (New York), *Tenth Anniversary Issue, 1948.*]

Nowadays, anyone who wishes to combat lies and ignorance and to write the truth must overcome at least five difficulties. He must have the *courage* to write the truth when truth is everywhere opposed; the *keenness* to recognize it, although it is everywhere concealed; the *skill* to manipulate it as a weapon; the *judgment* to select those in whose hands it will be effective; and the *cunning* to spread the truth among such persons. These are formidable problems for writers living under Fascism, but they exist also for those writers who have fled or been exiled; they exist even for writers working in countries where civil liberty prevails.

1. The Courage to Write the Truth

It seems obvious that whoever writes should write the truth in the sense that he ought not to suppress or conceal

truth or write anything deliberately untrue. He ought not
to cringe before the powerful, nor betray the weak. It is,
of course, very hard not to cringe before the powerful, and
it is highly advantageous to betray the weak. To displease
the possessors means to become one of the dispossessed.
To renounce payment for work may be the equivalent of
giving up the work, and to decline fame when it is offered
by the mighty may mean to decline it forever. This takes
courage.

Times of extreme oppression are usually times when
there is much talk about high and lofty matters. At such
times it takes courage to write of low and ignoble matters
such as food and shelter for workers; it takes courage when
everyone else is ranting about the vital importance of
sacrifice. When all sorts of honors are showered upon the
peasants it takes courage to speak of machines and good
stock feeds which would lighten their honorable labor.
When every radio station is blaring that a man without
knowledge or education is better than one who has studied,
it takes courage to ask: better for whom? When all the
talk is of perfect and imperfect races, it takes courage to
ask whether it is not hunger and ignorance and war that
produce deformities.

And it also takes courage to tell the truth about oneself,
about one's own defeat. Many of the persecuted lose their
capacity for seeing their own mistakes. It seems to them
that the persecution itself is the greatest injustice. The per-
secutors are wicked simply because they persecute; the
persecuted suffer because of their goodness. But this
goodness has been beaten, defeated, suppressed; it was
therefore a weak goodness, a bad, indefensible, unreliable
goodness. For it will not do to grant that goodness must
be weak as rain must be wet. *It takes courage to say that the
good were defeated not because they were good, but because they were weak.*

Naturally, in the struggle with falsehood we must write

the truth, and this truth must not be a lofty and ambiguous generality. When it is said of someone, "He spoke the truth," this implies that some people or many people or at least one person said something unlike the truth—a lie or a generality—but *he* spoke the truth, he said something practical, factual, undeniable, something to the point.

It takes little courage to mutter a general complaint, in a part of the world where complaining is still permitted, about the wickedness of the world and the triumph of barbarism, or to cry boldly that the victory of the human spirit is assured. There are many who pretend that cannon are aimed at them when in reality they are the target merely of opera glasses. They shout their generalized demands to a world of friends and harmless persons. They insist upon a generalized justice for which they have never done anything; they ask for a generalized freedom and demand a share of the booty which they have long since enjoyed. They think that truth is only what sounds nice. If truth should prove to be something statistical, dry, or factual, something difficult to find and requiring study, they do not recognize it as truth; it does not intoxicate them. They possess only the external demeanor of truth-tellers. The trouble with them is: *they do not know the truth.*

2. The Keenness to Recognize the Truth

Since it is hard to write the truth because truth is everywhere suppressed, it seems to most people to be a question of character whether the truth is written or not written. They believe that courage alone suffices. They forget the second obstacle: the difficulty of *finding* the truth. It is impossible to assert that the truth is easily ascertained.

First of all we strike trouble in determining *what* truth is worth the telling. For example, before the eyes of the whole world one great civilized nation after the other falls into barbarism. Moreover, everyone knows that the domestic war which is being waged by the most ghastly

methods can at any moment be converted into a foreign
war which may well leave our continent a heap of ruins.
This, undoubtedly, is one truth, but there are others. Thus,
for example, it is not untrue that chairs have seats and
that rain falls downward. Many poets write truths of this
sort. They are like a painter adorning the walls of a
sinking ship with a still life. Our first difficulty does not
trouble them and their consciences are clear. Those in
power cannot corrupt them, but neither are they disturbed
by the cries of the oppressed; they go on painting. The
senselessness of their behavior engenders in them a "pro-
found" pessimism which they sell at good prices; yet such
pessimism would be more fitting in one who observes these
masters and their sales. At the same time it is not easy to
realize that their truths are truths about chairs or rain;
they usually sound like truths about important things.
For it is the nature of artistic creation to confer importance.
But upon closer examination it is possible to see that
they say merely: a chair is a chair; and: no one can pre-
vent the rain from falling down.

They do not discover the truths that are worth writing
about. On the other hand, there are some who deal only
with the most urgent tasks, who embrace poverty and do
not fear rulers, and who nevertheless cannot find the truth.
These lack knowledge. They are full of ancient superstitions, with notorious prejudices that in bygone days were
often put into beautiful words. The world is too complicated
for them; they do not know the facts; they do not perceive
relationships. In addition to temperament, knowledge,
which can be acquired, and methods, which can be learned,
are needed. What is necessary for all writers in this age of
perplexity and lightning change is a knowledge of the
materialistic dialectic of economy and history. This knowledge can be acquired from books and from practical in-
struction, if the necessary diligence is applied. Many
truths can be discovered in simpler fashion, or at least

portions of truths, or facts that lead to the discovery of truths. Method is good in all inquiry, but it is possible to make discoveries without using any method—indeed, even without inquiry. But by such a casual procedure one does not come to the kind of presentation of truth which will enable men to act on the basis of that presentation. People who merely record little facts are not able to arrange the things of this world so that they can be easily controlled Yet truth has this function alone and no other. Such people cannot cope with the requirement that they write the truth.

If a person is ready to write the truth and able to recognize it, there remain three more difficulties.

3. The Skill to Manipulate the Truth as a Weapon

The truth must be spoken with a view to the results it will produce in the sphere of action. As a specimen of a truth from which no results, or the wrong ones, follow, we can cite the widespread view that bad conditions prevail in a number of countries as a result of barbarism. In this view, Fascism is a wave of barbarism which has descended upon some countries with the elemental force of a natural phenomenon.

According to this view, Fascism is a new, third power beside (and above) capitalism and socialism; not only the socialist movement but capitalism as well might have survived without the intervention of Fascism. And so on. This is, of course, a Fascist claim; to accede to it is a capitulation to Fascism. Fascism is a historic phase of capitalism; in this sense it is something new and at the same time old. In Fascist countries capitalism continues to exist, but only in the form of Fascism; and *Fascism can be combatted as capitalism alone, as the nakedest, most shameless, most oppressive, and most treacherous form of capitalism.*

But how can anyone tell the truth about Fascism, unless

he is willing to speak out against capitalism, which brings it forth? What will be the practical results of such truth?

Those who are against Fascism without being against capitalism, who lament over the barbarism that comes out of barbarism, are like people who wish to eat their veal without slaughtering the calf. They are willing to eat the calf, but they dislike the sight of blood. They are easily satisfied if the butcher washes his hands before weighing the meat. They are not against the property relations which engender barbarism; they are only against barbarism itself. They raise their voices against barbarism, and they do so in countries where precisely the same property relations prevail, but where the butchers wash their hands before weighing the meat.

Outcries against barbarous measures may be effective as long as the listeners believe that such measures are out of the question in their own countries. Certain countries are still able to maintain their property relations by methods that appear less violent than those used in other countries. Democracy still serves in these countries to achieve the results for which violence is needed in others, namely, to guarantee private ownership of the means of production. The private monopoly of factories, mines, and land creates barbarous conditions everywhere, but in some places these conditions do not so forcibly strike the eye. Barbarism strikes the eye only when it happens that monopoly can be protected only by open violence.

Some countries, which do not yet find it necessary to defend their barbarous monopolies by dispensing with the formal guarantees of a constitutional state, as well as with such amenities as art, philosophy, and literature, are particularly eager to listen to visitors who abuse their native lands because those amenities are denied there. They gladly listen because they hope to derive from what they hear advantages in future wars. Shall we say that they have recognized the truth who, for example, loudly demand an unrelenting struggle against Germany "because that country is now the true home of Evil in our day, the partner of hell, the abode of the Antichrist"? We should rather say that these are foolish and dangerous people. For the conclusion to be drawn from this nonsense is that since poison gas and bombs do not pick out the guilty, Germany must be exterminated—the whole country and all its people.

The man who does not know the truth expresses himself in lofty, general, and imprecise terms. He shouts about "the" German, he complains about Evil in general, and whoever hears him cannot make out what to do. Shall he decide not to be a German? Will hell vanish if he himself is good? The silly talk about the barbarism that comes out of barbarism is also of this kind. The source of barbarism is barbarism, and it is combatted by culture, which comes from education. All this is put in general terms; it is not meant to be a guide to action and is in reality addressed to no one.

Such vague descriptions point to only a few links in the chain of causes. Their obscurantism conceals the real forces making for disaster. If light be thrown on the matter it promptly appears that disasters are caused by certain men. For we live in a time when the fate of man is determined by men.

Fascism is not a natural disaster which can be understood simply in terms of "human nature." But even when we are dealing with natural catastrophes, there are ways to portray them which are worthy of human beings because they appeal to man's fighting spirit.

After a great earthquake that destroyed Yokohama, many American magazines published photographs showing heaps of ruins. The captions read: STEEL STOOD. And, to be sure, though one might see only ruins at first glance, the eye swiftly discerned, after noting the caption, that a few tall buildings had remained standing. Among the multitudinous descriptions that can be given of an earthquake, those drawn up by construction engineers concerning the shifts in the ground, the force of stresses, the heat developed, etc., are of the greatest importance, for they lead to future construction which will withstand earthquakes. If anyone wishes to describe Fascism and war, great disasters which are not natural catastrophes, he must do so in terms of a practical truth. He must show that these disasters are launched by the possessing classes to control the vast numbers of workers who do not own the means of production.

If one wishes successfully to write the truth about evil conditions, one must write it so that its avertible causes can be identified. If the preventable causes can be identified, the evil conditions can be fought.

4. The Judgment to Select Those in Whose Hands the Truth Will Be Effective

The century-old custom of trade in critical and descriptive writing and the fact that the writer has been relieved of concern for the destination of what he has written have caused him to labor under a false impression. He believes that his customer or employer, the middleman, passes on what he has written to everyone. The writer thinks: I have spoken and those who wish to hear will hear me. In reality he has spoken and those who are able to *pay* hear him. A great deal, though still too little, has been said about this; I merely want to emphasize that "writing for someone" has been transformed into merely "writing." But the truth cannot merely be written; it must be written *for someone,* someone who can do something with it. The process of recognizing truth is the same for writers and readers. In order to say good things, one's hearing must be good and one must hear good things. The truth must be spoken deliberately and listened to deliberately. And for us writers it is important to whom we tell the truth and who tells it to us. We must tell the truth about evil conditions to those for whom the conditions are worst, and we must also learn the truth from them. We must address not only people who hold certain views, but people who, because of their situation, should hold these views. And the audience is continually changing. Even the hangmen can be addressed when the payment for hanging stops, or when the work becomes too dangerous. The Bavarian peasants were against every kind of revolution, but when the war went on too long and the sons who came home found no room on their farms, it was possible to win them over to revolution.

It is important for the writer to strike the true note of truth. Ordinarily, what we hear is a very gentle, melancholy tone, the tone of people who would not hurt a fly. Hearing this one, the wretched become more wretched. Those who use it may not be foes, but they are certainly not allies. The truth is belligerent; it strikes out not only against falsehood, but against particular people who spread falsehood.

5. The Cunning to Spread the Truth
Among the Many

Many people, proud that they possess the courage necessary for the truth, happy that they have succeeded in finding it, perhaps fatigued by the labor necessary to put it into workable form and impatient that it should be grasped by those whose interests they are espousing, consider it superfluous to apply any special cunning in spreading the truth. For this reason they often sacrifice the whole effectiveness of their work. At all times cunning has been employed to spread the truth, whenever truth was suppressed or concealed. Confucius falsified an old, patriotic historical calendar. He changed certain words. Where the calendar read, "The ruler of Hun had the philosopher Wan killed because he said so and so," Confucius replaced *killed* by *murdered*. If the calendar said that tyrant so and so *died by assassination,* he substituted *was executed.* In this manner Confucius opened the way for a fresh interpretation of history.

In our times anyone who says *population* in place of *people* or *race*, and *privately owned land* in place of *soil*, is by that simple act withdrawing his support from a great many lies. He is taking away from these words their rotten, mystical implications. The word *people* (*Volk*) implies a certain unity and certain common interests; it should therefore be used only when we are speaking of a number of peoples, for then alone is anything like community of interest conceivable. The population of a given territory may have a good many different and even opposed interests— and this is a truth that is being suppressed. In like manner, whoever speaks of soil and describes vividly the effect of plowed fields upon nose and eyes, stressing the smell and color of earth, is supporting the rulers' lies. For the fertility of the soil is not the question, nor men's love for the soil, nor their industry in working it; what is of prime importance is the price of grain and the price of labor. Those who extract profits from the soil are not the same people who extract grain from it, and the earthy smell of a turned furrow is unknown on the produce exchanges. The latter have another smell entirely. *Privately owned land* is the right expression; it affords less opportunity for deception.

Where oppression exists, the word *obedience* should be employed instead of *discipline*, for discipline can be self-imposed and therefore has something noble in its character that obedience lacks. And a better word than *honor* is *human dignity;* the latter tends to keep the individual in mind. We all know very well what sort of scoundrels thrust themselves forward, clamoring to defend the honor of a people. And how generously they distribute honors to the starvelings who feed them. Confucius' sort of cunning is still valid today. Thomas More in his *Utopia* described a country in which just conditions prevailed. It was a country very different from the England in which he lived, but it resembled that England very closely, except for the conditions of life.

Lenin wished to describe exploitation and oppression on Sakhalin Island, but it was necessary for him to beware of the Czarist police. In place of Russia he put Japan, and in place of Sakhalin, Korea. The methods of the Japanese bourgeoisie reminded all his readers of the Russian bourgeoisie and Sakhalin, but the pamphlet was not blamed because Russia was hostile to Japan. Many things that cannot be said in Germany about Germany can be said about Austria.

There are many cunning devices by which a suspicious State can be hoodwinked.

Voltaire combatted the Church doctrine of miracles by writing a gallant poem about the Maid of Orleans. He described the miracles that undoubtedly must have taken place in order that Joan of Arc should remain a virgin in the midst of an army of men, a court of aristocrats, and a host of monks. By the elegance of his style, and by describing erotic adventures such as characterized the luxurious life of the ruling class, he threw discredit upon a religion which provided them with the means to pursue a loose life. He even made it possible for his works, in illegal ways, to reach those for whom they were intended. Those among his readers who held power promoted or tolerated the spread of his writings. By so doing, they were withdrawing support from the police who defended their own pleasures. Another example: the great Lucretius expressly says that one of the chief encouragements to the spread of Epicurean atheism was the beauty of his verses.

It is indeed the case that the high literary level of a given statement can afford it protection. Often, however, it also arouses suspicion. In such case it may be necessary to lower it deliberately. This happens, for example, when descriptions of evil conditions are inconspicuously smuggled into the despised form of a detective story. Such descriptions

would justify a detective story. The great Shakespeare deliberately lowered the level of his work for reasons of far
less importance. In the scene in which Coriolanus' mother
confronts her son, who is departing for his native city,
Shakespeare deliberately makes her speech to the son very
weak.* It was inopportune for Shakespeare to have Coriolanus restrained by good reasons from carrying out his
plan; it was necessary to have him yield to old habit with
a certain sluggishness.

Shakespeare also provides a model of cunning utilized
in the spread of truth: this is Antony's speech over Caesar's
body. Antony continually emphasizes that Brutus is an
honorable man, but he also describes the deed, and this
description of the deed is more impressive than the description of the doer. The orator thus permits himself to be
overwhelmed by the facts; he lets them speak for themselves.

An Egyptian poet who lived four thousand years ago
employed a similar method. That was a time of great class
struggles. The class that had hitherto ruled was defending
itself with difficulty against its great opponent, that part of
the population which had hitherto served it. In the poem
a wise man appears at the ruler's court and calls for struggle
against the internal enemy. He presents a long and impressive description of the disorders that have arisen from the
uprising of the lower classes. This description reads as
follows:

> So it is: the nobles lament and the servants rejoice.
> Every city says: Let us drive the strong from out of our

* Whether the speech is weak is questionable. And, if it
is weak, it is questionable whether this is deliberate. On
Brecht's interpretation of the Egyptian papyrus that follows,
see the footnote on the subject in my essay "An Un-American
Chalk Circle?" in *The Caucasian Chalk Circle* (2d printing;
rev. ed.; New York: Grove Press, 1967).—E. B.

midst. The offices are broken open and the documents removed. The slaves are becoming masters.

So it is: the son of a well-born man can no longer be recognized. The mistress's child becomes her slave girl's son.

So it is: The burghers have been bound to the millstones. Those who never saw the day have gone out into the light.

So it is: The ebony poor boxes are being broken up; the noble sesban wood is cut up into beds.

Behold, the capital city has collapsed in an hour.

Behold, the poor of the land have become rich.

Behold, he who had not bread now possesses a barn; his granary is filled with the possessions of another

Behold, it is good for a man when he may eat his food.

Behold, he who had no corn now possesses barns; those who accepted the largesse of corn now distribute it.

Behold, he who had not a yoke of oxen now possesses herds; he who could not obtain beasts of·burden now possesses herds of neat cattle.

Behold, he who could build no hut for himself now possesses four strong walls.

Behold, the ministers seek shelter in the granary, and he who was scarcely permitted to sleep atop the walls now possesses a bed.

Behold, he who could not build himself a rowboat now possesses ships; when their owner looks upon the ships, he finds they are no longer his.

Behold, those who had clothes are now dressed in rags, and he who wove nothing for himself now possesses the finest linen.

The rich man goes thirsty to bed, and he who once begged him for lees now has strong beer.

Behold, he who understood nothing of music now owns a harp; he to whom no one sang now praises the music.

Behold, he who slept alone for lack of a wife now has women; those who looked at their faces in the water now possess mirrors.

Behold, the highest in the land run about without

finding employment. Nothing is reported to the great any longer. He who once was a messenger now sends forth others to carry his messages....

Behold five men whom their master sent out. They say: go forth yourself; we have arrived.

It is significant that this is the description of a kind of disorder that must seem very desirable to the oppressed. And yet the poet's intention is not transparent. He expressly condemns these conditions, though he condemns them poorly....

Jonathan Swift, in his famous pamphlet, suggested that the land could be restored to prosperity by slaughtering the children of the poor and selling them for meat. He presented exact calculations showing what economies could be effected if the governing classes stopped at nothing.

Swift feigned innocence. He defended a way of thinking which he hated intensely with a great deal of ardor and thoroughness, taking as his theme a question that plainly exposed to everyone the cruelty of that way of thinking. Anyone could be cleverer than Swift, or at any rate more humane—especially those who had hitherto not troubled to consider what were the logical conclusions of the views they held.

Propaganda that stimulates thinking, in no matter what field, is useful to the cause of the oppressed. Such propaganda is very much needed. Under governments which serve to promote exploitation, thought is considered base.

Anything that serves those who are oppressed is considered base. It is base to be constantly concerned about getting enough to eat; it is base to reject honors offered to the defenders of a country in which those defenders go hungry; base to doubt the Leader when his leadership leads to misfortunes; base to be reluctant to do work that does not feed the worker; base to revolt against the compulsion to commit senseless acts; base to be indifferent to a family which can no longer be helped by any amount of concern.

The starving are reviled as voracious wolves who have nothing to defend; those who doubt their oppressors are accused of doubting their own strength; those who demand pay for their labor are denounced as idlers. Under such governments thinking in general is considered base and falls into disrepute. Thinking is no longer taught anywhere, and wherever it does emerge, it is persecuted.

Nevertheless, certain fields always exist in which it is possible to call attention to triumphs of thought without fear of punishment. These are the fields in which the dictatorships have need of thinking. For example, it is possible to refer to the triumphs of thought in fields of military science and technology. Even such matters as stretching wool supplies by proper organization, or inventing ersatz materials, require thinking. Adulteration of foods, training the youth for war—all such things require thinking; and in reference to such matters the process of thought can be described. Praise of war, the automatic goal of such thinking, can be cunningly avoided, and in this way the thought that arises from the question of how a war can best be waged can be made to lead to another question—whether the war has any sense. Thought can then be applied to the further question: how can a senseless war be averted?

Naturally, this question can scarcely be asked openly. Such being the case, cannot the thinking we have stimulated be made use of? That is, can it be framed so that it leads to action? It can.

In order that the oppression of one (the larger) part of the population by another (the smaller) part should continue in such a time as ours, a certain attitude of the population is necessary, and this attitude must pervade all fields A discovery in the field of zoology, like that of the Englishman Darwin, might suddenly endanger exploitation. And yet, for a time the Church alone was alarmed; the people noticed nothing amiss. The researches of physicists in recent years have led to consequences in the field of logic which might well endanger a number of the dogmas that keep oppression going. Hegel, the philosopher of the Prussian State, who dealt with complex investigations in the field of logic, suggested to Marx and Lenin, the classic exponents of the proletarian revolution, methods of inestimable value. The development of the sciences is interrelated, but uneven, and the State is never able to keep its eye on everything. The advance guard of truth can select battle positions which are relatively unwatched.

What counts is that the right sort of thinking be taught, a kind of thinking that investigates the transitory and changeable aspect of all things and processes. Rulers have an intense dislike for significant changes. They would like to see everything remain the same—for a thousand years, if possible. They would love it if sun and moon stood still.* Then no one would grow hungry any more, no one would want his supper. When the rulers have fired a shot, they do not want the enemy to be able to shoot; theirs must be the last shot. A way of thinking that stresses change is a good way to encourage the oppressed.

Another idea with which the victors can be confronted is that in everything and in every condition, a contradiction appears and grows. Such a view (that of dialectics, of the doctrine that all things flow and change) can be inculcated in realms that for a time escape the notice of the rulers. It can be employed in biology or chemistry, for example. But it can also be indicated by describing the fate of a family, and here too it need not arouse too much attention. The dependence of everything upon many factors which are constantly changing is an idea dangerous to dictators, and this idea can appear in many guises without giving the police anything to put their finger on. A complete description of all the processes and circumstances

---

* This line makes clearer than any other the relation of this essay to *Galileo*.—E. B.

encountered by a man who opens a tobacco shop can strike a blow against dictatorship. Anyone who reflects upon this will soon see why. Governments which lead the masses into misery must guard against the masses' thinking about government while they are miserable. Such governments talk a great deal about Fate. It is Fate, not they, which is to blame for all distress. Anyone who investigates the cause of the distress is arrested before he hits on the fact that the government is to blame. But it is possible to offer a general opposition to all this nonsense about Fate; it can be shown that Man's Fate is made by men.

This is another thing that can be done in various ways. For example, one might tell the story of a peasant farm— a farm in Iceland, let us say. The whole village is talking about the curse that hovers over this farm. One peasant woman threw herself down a well; the peasant owner hanged himself. One day a marriage takes place between the peasant's son and a girl whose dowry is several acres of good land. The curse seems to lift from the farm. The village is divided in its judgment of the cause of this fortunate turn of events. Some ascribe it to the sunny disposition of the peasant's young son, others to the new fields which the young wife added to the farm, and which have now made it large enough to provide a livelihood.

But even in a poem which simply describes a landscape something can be achieved, if the things created by men are incorporated into the landscape.

Cunning is necessary to spread the truth.

Summary

The great truth of our time is that our continent is giving way to barbarism because private ownership of the means of production is being maintained by violence. Merely to recognize this truth is not sufficient, but should it not be recognized, no other truth of importance can be discovered. Of what use is it to write something courageous which shows that the condition into which we are falling is barbarous (which is true) if it is not clear why we are falling into this condition? We must say that torture is used in order to preserve property relations. To be sure, when we say this we lose a great many friends who are against torture only because they think property relations can be upheld without torture, which is untrue.

We must tell the truth about the barbarous conditions in our country in order that the thing should be done which will put an end to them—the thing, namely, which will change property relations.

Furthermore, we must tell this truth to those who suffer most from existing property relations and who have the greatest interest in their being changed—the workers and those whom we can induce to be their allies because they too have really no control of the means of production even if they do share in the profits.

And we must proceed cunningly.

All these five difficulties must be overcome at one and the same time, for we cannot discover the truth about barbarous conditions without thinking of those who suffer from them; cannot proceed unless we shake off every trace of cowardice; and when we seek to discern the true state of affairs in regard to those who are ready to use the knowledge we give them, we must also consider the necessity of offering them the truth in such a manner that it will be a weapon in their hands, and at the same time we must do it so cunningly that the enemy will not discover and hinder our offer of the truth.

That is what is required of a writer when he is asked to write the truth.

—Translated by RICHARD WINSTON

APPENDIX B

Appendix B

ENGLISH TRANSLATIONS OF *GALILEO*

The first English translation of *Galileo* was probably the one made by Desmond I. Vesey in the late 1930's or very early 1940's. Mr. Vesey gave me a copy of his manuscript, which I subsequently placed in the Library of Kenyon College, Gambier, Ohio. It bore the title *The Star Gazer*. (I assumed the title was deliberately borrowed from Zsolt de Harsányi's "fictional biography" of Galileo, published in English in 1938, but Mr. Vesey informs me that it was an independent notion of his own. Brecht's own interest in Galileo may well have started with a reading of Harsányi, the German edition of which came out in 1937. However, the German edition was not called *The Star Gazer*.)

In the mid-1940's, an acting version of *Galileo* was prepared for Charles Laughton by two young American theatre men who were associated with Orson Welles: Brainerd Duffield and Emerson Crocker. In a letter, Mr. Duffield has told me that Brecht began by having a literal translation made by "a secretary." "But," Mr. Duffield continues, "we worked primarily from his German manuscript, aided by German dictionaries of argot and idioms, and frequently consulted refugee writers in the Hollywood colony for advice and opinion. Mr. Crocker comes from a German family but speaks no German, but I had four years of college German and had worked with Alfred Doeblin and other German writers at MGM That was the chief reason Laughton suggested me to Brecht for the job. Helli Brecht,

Salka Viertel, and others read the completed translation and said we had done an excellent job of catching Brecht's flavor, even to the puns and slang."

According to Mr. Duffield, the Laughton version was made from the Duffield-Crocker version with the help of Brecht. And, indeed, Brecht, in his notes on the play, has written of sitting with Laughton on the latter's Hollywood lawns and working on the project. A fascinating pluto-cratic-bucolic image! What creates a problem for the lit-erary historian is that Brecht makes no mention of any "secretary," any Duffield, or any Crocker, let alone of any Desmond Vesey, who had translated the whole play before any of these others went to work. When their names did not even appear in the program of the Hollywood produc-tion of the play, Messrs. Duffield and Crocker were re-portedly taken aback, and Orson Welles (I understand) sent a strong, perhaps even denunciatory telegram to Mr. Laughton. Far be it from me to try to disentangle the legal rights in this or any other Brechtian matter, but, from a purely literary point of view, it would be interesting to know how much of the version by the "secretary" sur-vived in the Duffield-Crocker text, and how much of the Duffield-Crocker survived in the Laughton. So far I have not been able to inspect the documents. Mr. Duffield no longer has a copy of his version. Mr. Crocker is not to be found. The Brecht Archive in East Berlin claims to have a copy of the Duffield-Crocker, but when I asked a young scholar to look up this and other points at the Archive, he was turned away empty-handed. To confuse matters further, if that is possible, the program of the 1947 production in New York adds this detail: "Lyrics adapted by Albert Brush."

What for better or for worse is always going to be called "the Laughton version" was first published in 1952 in my anthology *From the Modern Repertoire* (Volume II), and reprinted in *Seven Plays by Bertolt Brecht* in 1961. Desmond Vesey had by this time translated the final version of the German, as published by Suhrkamp Verlag (Frankfurt, 1957), and it is this translation which appears in the Methuen edition (London, 1960).

The present book represents the first separate publication of any version of *Galileo* in the United States, and in fact, up to now, only the Laughton version has appeared in this country either in print or on stage.

—E. B.